DIGITIZING MEDIEVAL MANUSCRIPTS

MEDIEVAL MEDIA CULTURES

Medieval Media Cultures offers analyses of how individuals interacted with written, visual, dramatic, and material media in medieval and early modern cultures, as well as how modern scholars interact with the remnants of medieval and early modern cultures via written, material, and now digital and electronic media.

This new series in media literacy welcomes proposals for monographs and essay collections in the fields of digital humanities, mapping, digital text analysis, games and gaming studies, literacy studies, and text production and interaction. We are especially interested in projects that demonstrate how digital methods and tools for research, preservation, and presentation influence the ways in which we interact with and understand these texts and media.

Series Editors

Toby Burrows, *University of Oxford*
Dorothy Kim, *Brandeis University*
Richard Utz, *Georgia Institute of Technology*

DIGITIZING MEDIEVAL MANUSCRIPTS

THE ST. CHAD GOSPELS, MATERIALITY, RECOVERIES, AND REPRESENTATION IN 2D AND 3D

BILL ENDRES

This work supported by a grant from the Vice President for Research of the University of Oklahoma.

British Library Cataloguing in Publication Data
A catalogue record for this book is available from the British Library

ISBN (PB): 9781802701227

www.arc-humanities.org
Printed and bound in the UK (by CPI Group [UK] Ltd), USA (by Bookmasters), and elsewhere using print-on-demand technology.

CONTENTS

LIST OF ILLUSTRATIONS

Figures

Tables

Introduction

THE AGE OF VISUAL WONDER: DIGITIZING MATERIALITY AND UNRIDDLING LIGHT

HOW A MANUSCRIPT reflects light changes over time. Folios become worn, damaged, and effaced. Humans make erasures, and more dramatically, wash or scrape away text to produce palimpsests. But also, there is the unrelenting hand of time, the gradual deterioration of inks and pigments, the slow discolouration and stiffening of parchment. Folios grow visually mysterious, like the enigmatic descriptions of common things in medieval riddles. Whether describing a wax tablet or an icicle, Aldhelm's riddles and those preserved in the Exeter Book tease readers with their baffling descriptions. As Patrick Murphy points out, Old English riddles start with phrases such as, "*wunderlicu wiht*, wondrous creature, something rich and strange," giving voice to an inanimate object and transforming it into a mysterious being.[1] As a folio ages, it too transforms into something rich and strange, turning into a *wunderlicu wiht*. Its lost pigments and ink make it an enigma waiting to be known.

Even for pages that have escaped severe damage, mysteries abound. There is much to be explored in the materiality of a manuscript. Pages are rich repositories of history: quality of parchment, types of pigments, wear from use, and markings from travels, all make manuscripts instructive witnesses to the medieval world and beyond. In the eighth-century St. Chad Gospels (Lich MS 1), the manuscript central to this study, enigmas exist about its damaged and erased text but also about its dry-point writing, the identity of its organic pigments, the number of artists and scribes who made it,[2] and even where it was made. As with fellow manuscripts from the Insular period (ca. 600–850, British Isles), few records survive, and even basic information, such as provenance, presents limited and misleading clues. But scholars have methods to coax knowledge from such limits. Paleographers urge insight by categorizing types of scripts and comparing the anatomy of letters. Codicologists explore layout, quires, and overall structures, revealing relations within a manuscript and correspondences among manuscripts and monasteries. Textual scholars study and trace biblical versions, and for early manuscripts such as the St. Chad Gospels, they have identified features such as recensions from Jerome's Vulgate to demonstrate traditions of texts and geographic relations among manuscripts. Like other scholarly approaches, advanced techniques of digital imaging have methods for teasing out insight. These methods labour with numerically captured visual information, making the page receptive to mathematical processing, moving beyond human capacities to unriddle mysteries held in reflected light.

---

1 Murphy, *Unriddling*, 7.
2 Endres, "Ligatures," 159–86.

To date, much of the focus of digital imaging has been on producing visual representations and increasing access. This is no trivial accomplishment. Projects such as e-Codices,[3] committed to digitizing and making available all medieval manuscripts in Switzerland, have transformed public access to and scholarly engagement with medieval manuscripts. Access and a simple tool, such as magnification, can lead to wondrous insight and revelation. However, this is only the initial wave of benefit. Further gains are possible from digital images taken with light frequencies beyond human vision, such as infrared and ultraviolet, an approach begun with photography in the first part of the twentieth century. Recently, for example, studying ultraviolet images, Myriah Williams and Paul Russell discovered two ghostly faces in the well-studied Black Book of Carmarthen (Peniarth MS 1, Llyfrgell Genedlaethol Cymru/The National Library of Wales).[4] Their discovery showcases the value of ultraviolet imaging for uncovering content otherwise lost in the shadows of an erasure. But again, this is only the beginning.

For digital imaging, innovative methods result from converting visual information into numerical values. This opens vast opportunities for analyzing manuscripts, many techniques readily available to medievalists. Once visual information becomes numeric, scholars can apply mathematical functions to manipulate and enhance it. Such methods can recover content from colour images, assess aging, and provide an enhanced view of surface details. Accessible to any medievalist, these approaches present countless benefits. For example, recovering content is possible without the need for ultraviolet or infrared imaging. Available methods can make recoveries even from photographs captured with a smartphone.[5] Therefore, when examining a manuscript at an archive, a scholar can take images and process them on site, able to assess digital recoveries by consulting the manuscript while it is still at hand.

But again, this is only the beginning. New 3D methods make studying the three-dimensional nature of a manuscript much more feasible. 3D renderings provide valuable visual information about the likes of the contours of pages, crucial for understanding trends in pigment loss. But furthermore, materiality is essential for interpretation. Scholars such as Jerome McGann and D. F. McKenzie recognize that reading is not an amorphous and passive experience, but rather a structured engagement with a palpable text.[6] With them, I celebrate the irreplaceable contributions of materiality to meaning. 2D photographs, for all their benefits, treat the page as a flat surface. They invite interpretation without input from attributes that require three-dimensional representation. Numerous scholars of manuscripts have critiqued this loss and expressed worries about training future scholars through examining 2D images, limiting contact with the rich three-dimensional nature of these bearers of medieval culture. Breakthroughs in 3D

---

3 e-Codices: www.e-codices.unifr.ch.

4 University of Cambridge Research, "Ghosts from the Past Brought Back to Life," www.cam.ac.uk/research/news/ghosts-from-the-past-brought-back-to-life.

5 Advanced imaging techniques are likely to produce much better results. Depending upon the damage, however, a processed image from a smartphone might provide a scholar with the needed details or enough details to make discoveries or justify an advanced imaging project.

6 McGann, *The Textual Condition*; McKenzie, *Bibliography*.

technologies, such as virtual reality, are opening possibilities for engaging manuscripts in new, multidimensional and multisensory ways.

While technologies matter, the guiding principle for digitizing a manuscript is a knowing engagement with its materiality. Materiality dictates which digital approaches provide the best potential for study and discovery. For any particular manuscript, no one technique can capture its complex materiality. For example, the St. Chad Gospels has required a collection of methods, methods for recovering damaged content, examining surface details, and studying the contours of pages. Complicating the conditions of its material features, the St. Chad Gospels, like most manuscripts, has had an eventful life, effecting its current state and needs when digitized. Having spent some of its early years in Wales, the manuscript has been known by various names, including St. Teilo Gospels, Llandeilo Fawr Gospels, Lichfield Gospels, and Book of St. Chad. It is a Latin gospel-book, likely made around 730 CE in Lichfield, England.[7] Its earliest known whereabouts is preserved in ninth-century marginalia, recording Gelhi, a Welshman, trading his best horse for the manuscript and presenting it to the Church of St. Teilo in Wales. This suggests that the gospel-book was stolen, likely for its cover, which would have been decorated with precious jewels and metals. Its travels and damage did not favour a long life. However, it has survived, its extant pages including the gospels of Matthew, Mark, and part of Luke, ending four words shy from completing Luke 3:9.

Generally, the most telling materiality concerns a manuscript's parchment, inks, and pigments. The pages of the St. Chad Gospels are vellum, that is, calfskin. It is of high quality, suggesting that the manuscript was made by an institution of substantial wealth. Roger Powell has estimated that it would have required 100 to 120 calves to make the original manuscript.[8] Although high quality, E. A. Lowe points out, "some leaves are greasy and very thick."[9] This greasiness might explain why some of the pigments have not adhered well, such as the yellow pigment orpiment. In contrast, the iron gall ink is in good shape except for water-damaged pages. Nevertheless, ink might dwell on the surface rather than penetrate into and bind with the vellum, boding ill for recoveries. Also, letters erased with a knife might likewise be unrecoverable. However, slight and irregular traces of water-damaged ink are visible, providing a favourable sign for some level of digital recovery.

The pigments of the St. Chad Gospels are noteworthy for a further reason. The St. Chad Gospels represents the oldest surviving Insular manuscript to exhibit extensively layered pigments. However, a substantial amount of pigment has been lost. Signs of this

---

7 Stein, *The Lichfield Gospels*; Brown, "The Lichfield Angel"; Brown, "The Lichfield/Llandeilo Gospels." Stein identifies Mercia and Northumbria as the most likely places for the making of the St. Chad Gospels, followed by Ireland and Wales. Brown provides cogent arguments for Lichfield, supported by recent research and the discovery of the Lichfield Angel in 2003. For an earlier, alternative perspective, see Jenkins and Owen, "The Welsh Marginalia," 41–56.

8 Powell, "The Lichfield," 261.

9 Lowe, *Codices Latini Antiquiores*, 12.

loss occur in the earliest photographs, which are from 1887, but a fair amount remains. Because pigments adhere to vellum and do not dye it, layered pigments are more susceptible, requiring stronger adhesion to remain on a page. Compounding this problem, the extent of early losses might signal that the binding material lacked the necessary strength, suggesting that remaining pigments survive at a greater risk. Therefore, leveraging digital imaging to discover and track trends in losses is crucial for conservation efforts and the longevity of this gospel-book.

The chapters in this book provide an analysis of materiality and digital imaging technologies; they describe the manner in which these imaging technologies *recover* and *preserve* materiality. The first three chapters focus on technologies for capturing various aspects of materiality. In Chapter 1, "Recovery: From Multispectral Imaging to Alternative Colour Spaces," I explore the benefits and limits of capturing reflected frequencies of light numerically. This includes the benefits of capturing frequencies outside of normal vision. I focus my discussion and examples on multispectral imaging (MSI), capable of capturing different frequencies of light, from ultraviolet, through the visual spectrum, and to infrared. To gain full benefits from these images, I assess approaches to post-processing, which are essential if images are generally going to produce more than cursory gains. However, regular colour images are not deprived of post-processing possibilities. These methods provide valuable recoveries for damaged and erased content. Therefore, I evaluate them, such as using alternative colour spaces, and develop an approach to what otherwise can be overwhelmingly complicated. Significantly, my approach includes processing photographs taken with a smartphone. I discuss and present these methods using open-source software. In this book, my goal is to make all of these digital methods accessible to and doable by any medievalist.

Chapter 2, "Reflectance Transformation Imaging: An Enhanced View of Surface Details" discusses one of my favourite advanced imaging techniques, referred to in short as RTI. RTI captures surface details, such as nearly impossible to see dry-point writing, etched with a stylus but no ink and meant to go unnoticed. I focus on highlight RTI, a method that uses a handheld flash to simulate a dome. RTI has proven highly valuable to archaeologists for recovering carvings in stone and other materials. However, RTI is equally as valuable for sorting out and discovering dry-point writing, for which scholars regularly report uncertainty in discerning its letters. Furthermore, I assess the value of RTI for other surface details, such as rising ink and pigment and viewing rulings and indentations from letters no longer visible.

Helping to preserve manuscripts might be the noblest contribution of digital images. They record how a manuscript presented itself, that is, reflected light, on a particular day, at a particular time, under particular lighting conditions, and to a particular beholder (including imaging technology conceived as a beholder of manuscripts). This recorded information remains, even as a manuscript ages. Although photography is a relatively new technology, earlier photographs (not much more than a century old) likewise record how a manuscript once presented itself. It is easy to think that new digital technologies capture more visual information; this is not always the case. A digital image cannot capture what a manuscript has lost through aging. In Chapter 3, "The Otherwise Unknowable: Digitizing and Comparing Historical Photographs," I provide a method for comparing digitized historical photographs with one another and with more recent digital images to discover trends in aging. This work includes digitizing historical photographs, using open-source software to align them, and a means (such as my overlay viewer or graphics editing software) to stack and compare them by adjusting transparency. Such work not only reveals trends in aging, but it also generates knowledge about the effects of past conservation treatments, such as the flattening of pages for the St. Chad Gospels. Furthermore, comparing historical images provides an opportunity to assess past photographic methods, highlighting surprising anomalies that increases critical awareness for all photographic methods. Ultimately, the chapter demonstrates the value and precision of early photographic techniques, including the photostat copy, and reveals that through the digital these historical photographs may well grow in value over time, contributing to issues such as aging, information otherwise beyond knowing.

The final two chapters address issues about the human element of digitization. In Chapter 4, "Sacred Artefacts: Open Access, Power, Ethics, and Reciprocity," I examine the significance of definitions, arguing that a manuscript that still serves its community is foremost a sacred artefact rather than an artefact of cultural heritage. This invites a turn to the ethnographic principle of reciprocity. Reciprocity provides beneficial guidance for scholarship, community interaction, and issues that emerge from open access and interdisciplinary collaboration. While advocating for open access, I address problems generated by it and a Creative Commons licensing agreement. I explore evolving copyright law and ambiguities connected to the transition from analogue to digital and print to the web. I argue that reciprocity aids with these difficulties, too. It provides guidance to foster strong relations even amid uncertainties and insure benefits for a community beyond unanticipated problems.

As the innovative media of their time, manuscripts generated awe and wonder: illuminated manuscripts represent the iMax movie of their day. They celebrated and cultivated the human capacity for wonder, and techniques—including those examined in detail throughout this book—are needed to restore this sense. I have long held that the Middle Ages is much more aptly described as the Age of Visual Wonder. In the digital age, 3D renderings help to translate this sense of awe, especially when the experience is provided through 3D flyovers. In Chapter 5, "A Crisis in Knowledge-Space? A Look Toward Virtual Reality," I assess 3D technologies and their renderings as a way to engage content as embodied. 2D photography, while dramatically increasing access, eliminates multidimensional features. To engage, assess, and develop virtual reality for manuscripts, I propose the concept of knowledge-space as a guide. To ground the concept, albeit brief and limited, I examine relied upon historical means for preserving and transmitting knowledge, beginning with the Greek dialectic, moving into the medieval manuscript, progressing to the book, and ending with the comparatively infant Web 2.0. This historical perspective highlights what I am calling "knowledge-spaces," culturally and ideologically constructed means for transmitting and preserving knowledge. It provides understanding of virtual reality as a new knowledge-space, helping to navigate its challenges and potentials for studying manuscripts.

In many ways, this book can be viewed as a critique of 2D photography. At conferences and in print, I have stated that scholars need to be more critically aware about the limits of 2D images, pointing to the example of some universities and colleges that consider photographs and even microfilm as primary sources. Doing so, not only overlooks their limits, but it also invites a forgetting that a page is a three-dimensional phenomenon, an organic substance that ages, that creaks and fusses when turned. Some features, such as the rise of layered pigments and contours of a page require three-dimensional techniques. But significantly, no one photograph captures THE scientific objective view. A manuscript is a play of light. Given technical decisions, each photograph highlights aspects of this play, thereby only aspects of a manuscript's materiality.

But critical assessment plays an even more crucial role. It is not an end in itself. It is only the beginning, the cornerstone of making in the digital humanities. Therefore, I view this book as a building upon the thinking, assessing, inventiveness, and countless hours of labour devoted to photography: from those labouring to invent and use the earliest forms to astrophysicists and their collaborators working to bring breakthroughs in digital imaging into the realm of manuscripts. I find the digital functions as a way to unify and celebrate these past efforts, perhaps no more clearly than my work uncovering trends in aging of the St. Chad Gospels, starting with photographs printed in an oversized 1887 book, through a photostat copy, through colour slides taken by Brother Frowin Oslender, through black-and-white photographs taken by the Courtauld Institute of Art, and to my multispectral imaging project in 2010. This book is about building upon the immeasurable labour, thinking, and ingenuity that began with the nineteenth-century invention of photography and the centuries of scholarship on manuscripts, the artists and scribes who laboured to make them, and the efforts to preserve them, including people such as Gelhi, for without whom the St. Chad Gospels would have been lost. Digitization is a way to celebrate the centuries of human achievement manifest in photography, scholarship, preservation, and manuscripts, build upon them to understand the past better, and in doing so, open otherwise unimagined potentials. This history itself, I believe, is a visual wonder worth recovering and preserving.

Chapter I

RECOVERY: FROM MULTISPECTRAL IMAGING TO ALTERNATIVE COLOUR SPACES*

"Colour is light embodied in a diaphanous medium. Indeed, this medium possesses two different qualities, for it is either pure, without the elements of earth, or impure, mixed with the elements of earth."

Robert Grosseteste (1168–1253)

METHODS OF RECOVERY have not always been kind to manuscripts. Concealing knowledge, damaged pages have long tantalized with traces of effaced script. To entice them to give up their secrets, reagents were applied, a practice which began at least in the seventeenth century but was more rigorously pursued in the nineteenth century.[1] The results, however, were disastrous. These chemicals, such as gallic acid and ammonium sulphide, were theorized to revitalize inks. Instead, they did so only temporarily, before turning a page into something less than its previous self: regularly a brown slur (Web Fig. 1.1).[2] Relying on the best knowledge of their day, such attempts remain a cautionary tale about the complex chemistry and fragility of the seemingly simple and common medieval materials of ink, pigment, and parchment.

Creating a theoretical frame for digital methods, early photography provided a means to recover damaged content through noninvasive techniques. It marked a critical turn from chemistry to physics, that is, recovery based on the properties of light.[3] Early experiments generated new methods, such as using orange lighting to increase contrast and coloured filters to reduce "the obscuring effects of stains."[4] More complex methods demonstrated further possibilities. For example, in the early twentieth century, Pringsheim and Gradeviss devised a method for recovering erased text from palimpsests.[5] This method required two film negatives: the first focused as sharply as possible on the erased script; the second focused equally on the two. To make the erased script more pronounced, Pringsheim and Gradeviss made a glass positive of the second negative (equal focus) and aligned and overlaid it with the negative focused on the

---

I Fuchs, "The History of Chemical," 161–63; Benton et al., "Digital Image-Processing," 41. Fuchs provides a recipe published by Petrus Maria Caneparius in *De Atramentis* (1619, Venice) of an extract of gall-nut in white wine to restore faded letters in antiquities. Benton et al. reference a Parisian notary named Raveneau who published a treatise in 1665 that recommends gallic acid for making faded or erased ink visible.

2 Fuchs, "The History of Chemical," 161–66; Benton et al., "Digital Image-Processing," 41–42; Mitchell and Hepworth, *Inks*, 130–31.

3 Benton et al., "Digital Image-Processing," 41–44.

4 Smith, "The Photography of Manuscripts," 191–92.

5 Mitchell and Hepworth, *Inks*, 132.

erased script. When examined under a light, the glass positive helped to neutralize the later writing, making traces of the erased script stand out. Such early techniques exemplify the overarching goal for recovery through noninvasive photographic methods: capitalize on properties of light to increase contrast, revealing that which has been lost to the unaided eye.

Building from film photography, digital imaging expands recovery possibilities. By numerically representing light, it introduces the power of computerized post-processing. This exponentially increases possibilities for recovery, avoiding limits caused by chemicals and developing film in a darkroom. Such computerized calculations once required the scientific knowledge of astrophysicists and support from organizations such as the US National Aeronautics and Space Administration (NASA); however, these methods are now readily available, some techniques executable on a smartphone. Through free open-source image-analysis software, such as ImageJ, complex and intricate recoveries can be done by any medievalist. Therefore, unprecedented opportunities exist to recover that which otherwise is lost.

In this chapter, I explore principles for guiding decisions about imaging choices for manuscripts. I examine imaging with nonvisible light, ultraviolet and infrared, and different frequencies of light in the visible spectrum. For recovering lost content, however, results from such imaging is only the beginning. Post-processing is regularly necessary. For such processing, I examine mathematical operations, merging alternative frequencies to generate an image, false colour, decorrelation, and alternative colour spaces. Because the sheer number of possibilities is daunting, I provide a method that produces initial results to guide recoveries. For the examples presented here I use images from the St. Chad Gospels. I focus on recoveries for water-damaged and erased content, comparing results for multispectral imaging and images from a high-resolution colour camera. While multispectral imaging provides more possibilities, post-processing of colour images likewise can produce excellent results, even when images are taken with a smartphone. I demonstrate that while knowing different options for advanced imaging technologies is helpful, understanding the properties of light and the materiality of the manuscript are essential for guiding imaging choices and recovery processes.

Decisions and Methods

No matter the approach to digital imaging, methods for recovery are available. Two aspects, however, are key: understanding the materiality of a manuscript and understanding the properties of light. Light is constructed from a spectrum of frequencies. They vary in wavelengths. As demonstrated by a prism, these frequencies can be separated, producing the colours of the rainbow. The human eye is generally sensitive to wavelengths measuring from 380 to 700 nm (nanometre, one billionth of a metre). Advanced images techniques such as multispectral imaging (MSI) and hyperspectral imaging (HSI) capture individual bands of light reflected by a page. The same principles guide both technologies. For example, the relatively new HSI captures the complete spectrum for each pixel, but generally breaks it into twenty to upward of three hundred bands. It builds upon MSI, which captures roughly six to thirteen narrow and intermittent bands, such as specific frequencies for ultraviolet, blue, green, yellow, orange, red, and infrared.[6] For the St. Chad Gospels, I used MSI, generally capturing thirteen frequencies. I will focus my discussion on it. Although HSI provides increased data and possibilities for recoveries, there is no guarantee it will produce better results. Recoveries depend on the material features of a manuscript and their condition. They affect reflected light and determine the best suited digital approach.[7]

One of the foremost benefits of MSI is extending human vision. It can capture unseen frequencies of reflected light and make their patterns visible. For manuscripts, capturing ultraviolet and infrared wavelengths has produced significant gains. Applying such approaches was underway at the beginning of the twentieth century. Experiments demonstrated that infrared was adept for recovering carbon-based inks whereas ultraviolet proved beneficial for recovering iron gall.[8] Both types of recoveries depend on parchment reflecting substantial amounts of nonvisible light while different inks absorb it, that is, carbon-based inks absorb infrared whereas iron gall absorbs ultraviolet. This generates the needed contrast to view the otherwise indiscernible remains of script. By the 1930s, a range of lighting and photographic equipment were available and producing good results, revealing damaged content for such works as the Leiden Riddle (Codex Voss 106, Leiden University), Ælfred's Boethius, (Cotton MS Otho V. vii, British Museum), and Beowulf manuscript (Cotton MS Vitellius A. xv, British Library).[9]

Modern methods build on these early approaches and experimentations. For example, prior to the outbreak of World War I, to recover the effaced text of palimpsests, Dom Kögel pioneered ultraviolet fluorescence.[10] His technique extends the benefits of nonvisible light. When parchment and other organic materials absorb ultraviolet light, they reemit it at slightly longer and visible wavelengths, making them glow. Alternatively, minerals such as iron, and consequently iron gall ink, absorb and do not reemit it. When parchment fluoresces, it generates greater contrast between it and nonvisible traces of effaced ink, revealing damaged text.[11,12]

The St. Chad Gospels creates two types of challenges for digital recovery. First, the manuscript contains water-damaged content. Some of the pages include faint traces of

---

6 For a comparison of HSI and MSI, see George et al., "A Study of Spectral Imaging," 141–58.

7 For recoveries in manuscripts, uses of HSI are growing. It has produced excellent results in revealing damaged imagery in the Mesoamerican codex MS. Arch. Seldon. A. 2. See Snijders et al., "Using Hyperspectral Imaging."

8 Haseldens, *Scientific Aids*, 70–73; Smith, "The Photography of Manuscripts," 191–96.

9 Smith, "The Photography of Manuscripts," 197–200.

10 Benton et al., "Digital Image-Processing," 42–43.

11 Fluorescence photography needs to occur in the dark, with a filter to block out other frequencies of light except the fluorescence (Haseldens, *Scientific Aids*, 71–72).

12 Unfortunately, if parchment has been treated with a reagent, it loses its ability to fluoresce.

or nonvisible text. Although the gospels are a version of the Vulgate,[13] variations exist and are significant for understanding doctrine and sources for the text. Nine pages have significant amounts of undiscernible script on multiple lines: pages 90, 91, 112, 113, 157, 192, 193, 204, and 216. Page 90 represents a good range of damage and serves as my primary example (Web Fig. 1.2).

Likewise, water has damaged pigments. Generally, pigments present more difficulty for recovery than inks. Inks etch into parchment, forming a molecular bond, whereas pigments adhere to it. Pigments that break free, therefore, leave less of a trace. For the St. Chad Gospels, the most extreme case of damaged pigments occurs on the first extant page, the incipit of Matthew. In the early years, it likely served as the outer cover of the manuscript.[14] This page suffers from water damage, but it also suffers from severe wear, rubbing against a countless number of objects and human hands when carried about. In this book I examine digital recovery for this incipit (Web Fig. 1.2) but also for the portrait and incipit of Mark, adjoining pages that have a representative range of pigment loss (Web Fig. 1.3).

The second type of recovery, scribal erasures, presents challenges because scribes scraped away unwanted text with a knife. Generally, such scraping results in less residue than with water damage or the effaced text of a palimpsest. For palimpsests, methods of effacing vary, including rubbing with powdered pumice and scraping with a pumice stone or knife. Because multiple and whole pages are effaced, the effort is generally less focused than with a single letter, word, or sentence. In the St. Chad Gospels, larger erasures occur on pages 3 and 196, but individual erased letters occur on a number of pages, including pages 11, 37, 59, and 78. Pages 3, 37, and 78 provide a representative sample (Web Fig. 1.4). Whereas such corrections characterize typical scribal activity, erasures can provide significant clues about transcription practices and competing versions of the text.

For the St. Chad Gospels, however, a more substantial erasure occurs on page 141. It appears to be an erased memorandum. This page contains highly significant marginalia, and not simply for the St. Chad Gospels. It includes some of the earliest examples of Old Welsh writing. One of these entries provides the first record of the whereabouts of the St. Chad Gospels. The page is framed and contains the last eight lines of Matthew's gospel, centred in the middle. Within the frame are two mixed Old Welsh/Latin memorandums and a list of Anglo-Saxon names (Web Fig. 1.5). Likely dating from the ninth century, the upper entry records the Welshman Gelhi trading his best horse for the manuscript and presenting it for the good of his soul to the Church of St. Teilo at Llandeilo Fawr, Wales.

The second entry, known by its first word as the *Surexit* entry, records a land dispute, but its arrangement is peculiar. The whole of this entry does not fit in the space above the

---

13 In 382, Pope Damasus requested that Jerome revise the Bible into a standard Latin version. At the time, a variety of versions, known as Old Latin, were in circulation. Pope Damasus not only desired a standard version of the Bible, but he also desired it in common Latin rather than the classical Latin of Cicero, favoured in the Old Latin texts.

14 Brown, "The Lichfield/Llandeilo," 64.

text of Matthew's gospel; the scribe wrote its final part in the bottom third of the space below. This second part appears after the erased entry and a later listing of Anglo-Saxon names. Why this entry does not appear immediately after the erasure is odd. Adding further peculiarity, scholars generally believe it to be the eldest marginalia; the Gelhi entry is believed to have been copied later, perhaps from a lost page.[15] This raises questions about why its placement is not directly below the upper frame and before the concluding lines of Matthew's gospel or the complete entry copied after them. Therefore, recovering any text from this erasure could aid in sorting out these questions and provide new insight into the early years of the St. Chad Gospels.

Given the importance of this erasure, I would have preferred fluorescence imaging. Fluorescence has proven beneficial where other methods have failed.[16] However, digitizing rarely occurs under ideal circumstances. For the MSI portion of my imaging, I had less than six months to pull together the project. Partial funding resulted from the unfortunate death of Ross Scaife, a well-known digital humanities and classics professor, the sole humanities faculty on a large grant attempting to digitally unroll damaged scrolls. After his death, the computer scientist was stumped for a solution to distinguish the text from the papyri. Rather than return funding, he instead approached another classics professor and friend to attempt a project digitizing a manuscript. This professor experienced difficulties securing a project, and the computer scientist turned to me.

In a perfect world, one imaging approach would capture every material aspect of a manuscript, but alas, no one magic solution exists. Materiality is too complex. If I had had more time, I would have lined up fluorescence expertise.[17] Although the computer scientist lacked this capability, he had a monochrome camera for MSI (MegaVision E6, 39-megapixal sensor).[18] MSI would provide multiple options for recovery, nearly certain to make some recoveries possible for water-damaged text. Also, it would provide significant information for the whole manuscript and invaluable information for future imaging possibilities. Although doubtful about prospects for page 141, I was hopeful MSI would provide some hints about its mystery.

---

15 Jenkins and Owen, "The Welsh Marginalia," 56–61.

16 The value of fluorescence was evident in the pioneering work of Dom Kögel. A. H. Smith discusses some early successes with recoveries for the *Leiden Riddle*, Aelfred's *Boethius*, and *Beowulf* manuscript (Smith, "The Photography of Manuscripts," 197–200). For an example of contemporary recoveries and systems, see Easton et al., "Standardized system for multispectral imaging of palimpsests." For fluorescence through HSI, see Shiel et al., "The Ghost in the Manuscript: Hyperspectral Text Recovery and Segmentation."

17 For a more complete account of the project and the significant efforts of Lichfield Cathedral and Canon Chancellor Pete Wilcox, see https://lichfield.ou.edu/content/acknowledgements.

18 For fluorescence imaging, I would have needed to purchase the proper filter and learned the technique. Having less than six months was challenging. I barely had time to work out the details for the project, including the contract, which arrived at Lichfield signed by my institution (via overnight shipping) on the morning of the first scheduled day of imaging.

Overall, MSI was a good choice. Nonvisible wavelengths had never been captured for the St. Chad Gospels. Infrared and ultraviolet frequencies would provide a previously unseen view of the manuscript and additional options for recoveries through post-processing. However, the drawback for ultraviolet is that it damages organic material. This damage is witnessed in the gradual darkening of parchment. To minimize such damage, systems such as MegaVision use LED lighting. This minimizes damage by emitting only the frequency necessary for an image. However, LED lighting requires total darkness so that other light does not pollute the results, a challenge in a thirteenth-century cathedral. Although LED lighting minimizes exposure, the conservator was cautious about exposing the manuscript to ultraviolet. Consequently, not every page has an ultraviolet image. This was in part because Roger Powell had used liquid nylon to improve consolidation of pigments; liquid nylon yellows with time. Although Powell's method involved placing tiny portions below rising pigment, the conservator wished to take every precaution. Therefore, I made scholarly arguments while imaging, when a page was before us and we could examine it, justifying, or not, an ultraviolet image.

To provide ample frequencies for recovery, a variety of visible and nonvisible frequencies were chosen. Because of damage caused by ultraviolet light, only 365 nm was captured at a short interval. In the visible range, I captured 450, 465 (blue), 505, 535 (green), 592, 625, 638 (red), and 700 nm. Infrared frequencies do not damage inks, pigments, or parchment. Therefore, I captured multiple: 730, 780, 850, and 940 nm. Infrared penetrates below the surface. Because the artists of the St. Chad Gospels layered pigments, seeing into these layers and below them could reveal valuable information, including underdrawings that might provide information about artistic processes and relations to practices found in other manuscripts.

But a major advantage of digital photography is increased options for post-processing. These methods are similar, whether regular colour or monochrome camera. To compare recovery for regular colour and MSI, I include post-processing of images taken with a high-resolution colour camera by the British Library in 2003. I target two types of post-processing: mathematical operations and alternative colour spaces. Mathematical operations, such as subtraction and division, can work well to reveal subtle patterns. While a digital image provides the illusion of looking at a page in a manuscript, it is made up of pixels, each with a numerical value. For an 8-bit greyscale image, reflected light is numerically recorded for each pixel from 0 to 255, black to white. For a colour image, each pixel has a value for red, green, and blue, ranging from 0 to 255. More subtleties are provided by 16-bit images, with values ranging from 0 to 65535. If bleed-through interferes with traces of damaged content, subtracting one image from another can sometimes reduce this distraction and increase contrast for damaged content. However, I have found best results with division. Division amplifies small differences without losing content. If successful, resulting values for bleed-through and parchment approach a value of 1 (near black), whereas traces of ink attain different values, making them visible.

For mathematical operations and recoveries, ImageJ provides a robust solution.[19] Funded by the US National Institute of Health (NIH), ImageJ is free, open-source software

---

19 Schindelin et al., "The ImageJ Ecosystem."

for medical image analysis. A benefit of using a medical solution is that medical imaging is at the forefront of digital techniques. To accommodate innovations, ImageJ has an open architecture, making plugins easy to development and install. Plugins, therefore, are generally available for the latest technologies and methods. Making all of these plugins easier to manage, ImageJ also provides downloadable versions with plugins preloaded. For manuscripts, Fiji provides a good range of options for post-processing images, including those for registration, discussed in Chapter 3.[20]

When coupled with ImageJ, MSI generates an abundance of riches for recoveries. However, this abundance can be overwhelming. Thirteen images of different frequencies of light provide 78 possibilities alone for dividing images, not to mention an additional 78 if the dividend and divisor are reversed. The St. Chad Gospels has 236 pages. Because of such abundance, I begin with an approach to gain an overview for potential recoveries, that is, determine which light frequencies vary in such a way that they might provide opportunities to reveal damaged content. For this, I divide the RGB image by its red, green, and blue frequency. Then, I divide it by the ultraviolet and an infrared frequency not too far into the infrared range (too far and the wavelength penetrates too extensively into the parchment). Although this is not a definitive approach, its results provide a means to expose frequencies apt for generating desired contrast.

Initially, mathematical operations might produce images of near blackness. For example, when dividing two images, resulting pixels regularly do not exceed a value of 4 or 5. But because the numeric distribution of an 8-bit image can range from 0 to 255, these values can be stretched over the full 255 range, dramatically increasing contrast. In graphics editing software, this adjustment is made through the histogram, which presents the distributed values of pixel in a graph. In ImageJ, adjustments to the histogram occur through the *Brightness/Contrast* tool under *Image > Adjust*. The *Maximum* slider keeps zero values at zero while stretching all of the other values. Therefore, the blackest pixels remain black while blackish-grey pixels are stretched into the whitish realm, making unseen patterns emerge.

Mathematical operations are invaluable, but they are not limited to images captured through MSI. Colour digital photographs are generated by merging red, green, and blue light, meriting their name: RGB images. In 1862, James Clerk Maxwell first demonstrated this possibility, its theory and mathematics well equipped for digital cameras. Normally, a digital camera has a Bayer filter over its sensor. Using a pattern, it filters light, allowing only red, green, or blue frequencies to reach any one of the photodetectors of a camera's sensor. Software in the camera merges the captured red, green, and blue frequencies into a colour image. By contrast, for MSI done with a monochrome camera, each photodetector captures the frequency of light that enters the lens for a pixel. Therefore, during final-processing, red, green, and blue images must be merged to create a colour image. For the St. Chad Gospels, I merged images of red (638 nm), green (535 nm), and blue (465 nm).

Because colour cameras produce an RGB image, it does not mean that individual frequencies of light are lost. Because the math is known for merging red, green, and blue

---

20 Fiji: http://imagej.net/Fiji/Downloads.

frequencies, the same math can be reversed and applied to separate them. Such splitting divides a colour photograph into its red, green, and blue channels, rendering each as a separate image. Programs such as ImageJ provide this functionality: *Image > Colour > Split Channels*. Once a colour photograph is split into red, green, and blue images, they can be divided into or subtracted from one another or the colour image, providing the potential for recoveries. For success, one of the channels must capture more data for traces of damaged content, providing the opportunity to generate contrast. Compared to MSI, splitting colour photographs provides a limited number of frequencies—three—for mathematical operations; however, it can still produce beneficial results.

For RGB images, the second type of recovery provides more possibilities. Again, it takes advantage of mathematically representing light, but this time, the method expresses the elements of colour differently, through alternative colour spaces. Alternative colour spaces originate from work by the *Commission Internationale de l'Eclairage* (CIE), a scientific organization dedicated to developing standards for colour. In 1931, CIE introduced CIE XYZ, a tristimulus model for colour based on human vision, capable of representing theoretical colours within the visual range. Tristimulus models generate full colour by merging three channels. CIE XYZ is similar to RGB, but the Y value (green) contains a factor for luminance, a factor contained in each channel for RGB. However, colour spaces are not limited in their channels to red, green, and blue. They can represent values for different elements of colour. For example, the HSV/HSB colour space represents colour as a combination of hue, saturation, and brightness.[21]

Because these channels represent elements of reflected light differently, they provide potential for revealing unseen patterns. As mentioned, the HSV/HSB model represents colour as a combination of hue, saturation, and brightness. When an image is separated into each of these elements, different information for reflected light becomes visible, opening the possibility for unseen patterns to emerge. In a colour image, bleed-through is largely visible because its brightness and hue varies from the surrounding parchment. Separate brightness and hue into their own channels, and in the remaining channel, saturation, bleed-through fades into the parchment. With its effect diminished or eliminated, contrast is potentially created for other patterns, such as traces of damaged text, unriddling its light.

Colour scientists have generated a multitude of alternative colour models for various needs, from sending television signals to storing video. To separate colour images into their components, ImageJ provides an easy to use and reliable plugin: Colour Transformer 2. Developed by Maria E. Barilla at the University of Birmingham, UK, it provides conversions for twenty-one different colour spaces. Each space has the potential to reveal valuable and/or subtle visual information; however, a number of the

---

21 Because each colour is expressed by three values, a visual rendering of these colour models is three-dimensional, each colour represented by a point within a geometric shape. Therefore, these models are known as colour spaces, mathematically forming shapes such as cubes, cones, and spheres. The shape is determined by mathematical relations among values, represented in different models through various linear or nonlinear means.

models are similar. Therefore, as a method, I begin with five models that provide a range of alternatives. Once I attain good results, if necessary, I rely on similar models to try to enhance them.

For initial conversions, these models provide a good variety of alternatives: Lab, YIQ, HSV/HSB, HCY, and CMYK. Normally, I begin with Lab. Lab mathematically represents colour by combining L (lightness or luminance) with two values for colour (chromaticity), a and b. Lightness is represented on a scale from 1 to 100, from black to white. The two chromaticity variables, a and b, represent values for colour along two different axes: a along red–green and b along blue–yellow. Although patterns represented by lightness are generally viewable in a regular colour image, Lab's chromaticities provide alternative patterns in two ways: first, they represent frequencies of light without information for luminous; and, second, they represent colours on axes constructed of two colours rather than as values for one of three.

Generating an alternative to Lab, the YIQ colour model represents chromaticity at a slant. It rotates the colour axes of Lab by 33 degrees. The I of YIQ indicates values for colours along an orange–blue axis; the Q indicates colours along a purple–green axis. By presenting colour information differently, YIQ provides visual information that potentially generates patterns of reflected light previously unseen.

Two related models, HCY and the already mentioned HSV/HSB, provide further possibilities. In the latter, V (value) or B (brightness) represent luminance. H provides a value for hue. Hue generally does not prove beneficial; its patterns reflect those of colour in colour photographs. However, S (saturation) regularly does. In HSV/HSB, saturation is represented as a value indicating the dilution of a hue by white. If this value is higher for traces of damaged ink than for parchment and bleed-through, the S-channel generates contrast and the damaged text emerges.

The related model, HCY, provides an alternative representation for saturation. Also, Y (luminosity) is calculated slightly differently than V and B of HSV/HSB. However, the value of C (chroma) proves more beneficial. This value represents purity of colour, calculated as the difference of the hue from the nearest grey. Because this calculation provides different values than the dilution of white in S of HSV/HSB, HCY poses a new possibility for generating contrast and revealing traces of lost content.

In testing for recovery, my final colour space is not tristimulus. It is a subtractive model that contains four values: CMYK. C provides a value for cyan, M for magenta, Y for yellow, and K for black. This model was developed for printing. Because of the difficulty in generating a pure black from cyan, magenta, and yellow, CMYK contains a separate value for it. CMYK provides an easily overlooked potential for recovery that can produce surprising results.

Patterns emerging from alternative colour spaces can be subtle. Whether revealing traces of a descender through the dilution of white or the cross-stroke of a t through a different chromaticity, sorting them out can be visually demanding. However, contrast can be enhanced through false colour. False colour emphasizes subtleties by applying contrasting colours to faint variations. It requires changing the colour lookup table, commonly called a *lut*. Luts are indices used to map colours to pixels. An alternative mapping transforms an image from realistic to colours highlighting subtle and not so subtle distinctions. ImageJ makes applying luts simple: *Image > Lookup Table*. Lookup Table lists roughly fifty different luts, designed to contrast different subtleties or aspects within colours. As with all methods of digital recovery, experimenting is key to enhance contrast.

One final approach is worth mentioning: DStretch, a plugin for ImageJ.[22] It recovers lost content through yet another mathematical method, decorrelation stretch. Developed by NASA's Jet Propulsion Lab, decorrelation applies an algorithm to increase the contrasts within colours, bringing out subtle differences. Mathematician John Harman developed DStretch for recovering rock art; therefore, it is adept at revealing reds, greens, and yellows. However, Harman provides a number of pre-sets, slide-bars for tailoring adjustments, and an *Expert* option for customized results. This makes DStretch flexible and viable for manuscripts.

Since the 1970s, digital methods have made astounding advances. In those early years, supported by NASA and its funds for applying "space technology to terrestrial uses," John Benton, Alan R. Gillespie, and James Soha used an electric camera and digital post-processing to recover the erased *ex-libris* in a fourteenth-century manuscript.[23] They demonstrated the promise of digital methods, inspiring Kevin Kiernan to pursue his innovative work on the Beowulf manuscript (British Library, Cotton MS Vitellius A. xv). In the 1980s, working with the British Library and their Video Spectral Comparator (video was the standard approach for digital sensors developed for satellites), Kiernan pushed further into the possible. A step in his method remains crucial today: no matter the results from digital methods of recovery, consult the manuscript, or if not possible, high-quality colour photographs. As Kiernan explains, colour makes evident localized discolourations that can clarify areas that otherwise lead to misinterpretation.[24] Today, results from a variety of methods can be compared as one form of confirmation. However, limits still exist. Kiernan's step is as sound today as it was to his digital recoveries: make every effort to consult the manuscript, and if not, consult high-quality colour photographs.

Results and Discussion

All recovery methods, whether dividing frequencies, alternative colour spaces, or decorrelation stretch, proved beneficial for at least some lost content. Although all methods routinely made water-damaged text emerge, dividing frequencies of light regularly clarified it. Likewise, but less consistently, methods recovered erased text and lost pigments. Alternative colour spaces made the extent of original pigments, such as orpiment, more evident. For erasures, methods recovered individual letters and the erased line on page 3. The marginalia on page 141, however, proved resistant. Yet, methods revealed that a portion of the erasure is imagery. Using either 16-bit

---

22 DStretch: www.dstretch.com.

23 Benton et al., "Digital image-processing," 40n1.

24 Kiernan, "Digital Image Processing," 20.

TIFs or 8-bit JPGs produced solid recoveries, with 16-bit TIFs revealing subtleties, representing values of colour on a scale from 0 to 65,535 rather than 0 to 255. But good results obtained from JPGs bode well when recovering content from images taken with a smartphone.

To organize results, I first examine recovery methods for water-damaged and worn text. I proceed to erasures and page 141, and I end with alternative colour spaces for examining damaged pigments. Applying these methods demonstrates that images generated by MSI provide greater flexibility and leverage for recovering that which is otherwise lost.

Recovery of Water-Damaged and Worn Text

As mentioned, page 90 presents a range of challenges for recovering water-damaged text. To assess methods and imaging, I apply the same methods to two RGB images: one taken by a high-resolution colour camera by the British Library in 2003, and the other by a monochrome camera by Bill Endres in 2010. I limit examples to the beginning of the first two lines because they provide an efficient range of damage. Placing the images side-by-side, however, reveals a subtle but important beginning difference: the parchment in the 2010 image appears greyer (Web Fig. 1.6). Examining colour histograms for each image affirms this observation. Proportionally, the 2010 image contains more grey, produced by a larger overlap of red, green, and blue frequencies (Fig. 1.1 or Web Fig. 1.7). This difference affects recovery.

Digital photography is not an exact science. For different digital images, the values for pixels vary. This causes the shapes of histograms to vary. For the 2010 image, the graphed values for red, green, and blue are wider, affecting overlap. Valleys and peaks show slightly different shapes. Such differences occur because even in high-end cameras, the sensitivity of sensors and their calibrated software differ. But filters also cause

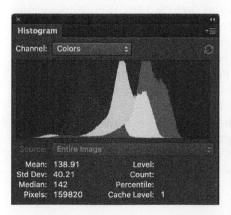 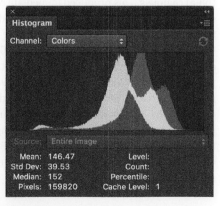

Figure 1.1. Histograms for beginning of first two lines, page 90, St. Chad Gospels. Left: High-resolution colour image. Right: Image merging 638 nm, 535 nm, and 465 nm frequencies.

variations. A colour digital camera has a Bayer filter blocking all frequencies except the red, green, or blue desired for each photodetector. The sensitivity of these filters fluctuates, requiring differently calibrated software to merge frequencies and produce a colour image that is realistic to the human eye. For MSI, when LED lighting is used, however, filters are unnecessary. This eliminates a significant variable. Therefore, different cameras produce images that record different values for reflected light. This causes histograms to differ, but importantly, it causes the success of digital recovery to vary.

For page 90, images taken with MSI for nonvisible frequencies produce, at best, minor recoveries. Ultraviolet light generates the best results. It increases the visibility of remnants of letters written in iron gall ink, the iron absorbing it while surrounding parchment reflects more of it (Fig. 1.2 or Web Fig. 1.8).[25] Furthermore, because parchment reflects more ultraviolet light than penetrates to the bleed-through text, bleed-through fades. However, parchment darkened by water-damage diminishes this positive gain. Darkened parchment absorbs more ultraviolet light. Contrast, therefore, increases only faintly. While recoveries are marginal, they indicate proportional differences for values of pixels. This suggests that dividing images of visible and nonvisible frequencies can enhance traces of ink and reveal patterns for damaged text, significant for the first line, still riddled in mystery.

Confirming that ink is not carbon-based, infrared frequencies provide no additional information. For example, the image for 850 nm makes remnants of damaged text disappear. Its longer wavelengths pass through them, moving recovery in the wrong direction (Web Fig. 1.9). As mentioned, iron gall ink does not absorb infrared light as carbon-based inks do; consequently, they are initially unbeneficial for increasing contrast. However, the ability of infrared frequencies to capture more bleed-through than damaged ink presents an opportunity. Through mathematical operations, they provide another possible way to generate contrast.

To attempt recovery and identify further frequencies for mathematical operations, I divided the RGB multispectral image by its 638 nm (red), 535 nm (green), and 465 nm (blue) channels. This produced immediate results (Web Fig. 1.10). All three dramatically decrease the interference caused by bleed-through; however, dividing by 465 nm makes the damaged text on the first line emerge most clearly: *tori suo* (Web Fig. 1.11). The Latin Vulgate affirms this recovery. Page 90 begins by concluding Matthew 20:8, a parable about labourers starting their work at fluctuating times but all receiving identical pay. The expected Vulgate words are *procuratori suo* (his steward). Page 89 ends with *procura*; therefore, *tori* completes this word. The *suo* is evident in all three results, most clearly in the RGB image divided by 465 nm. Through further division, 465 nm shows promise for refining recoveries or producing them for other pages with water-damaged text. However, results from 638 nm and 535 nm also show promise. They could prove effective in different combinations. Therefore, images from MSI provide an excess of possibilities for producing recoveries.

---

25 Part of the reflected light is parchment fluorescing, the effect that Dom Kögel realized could be harnessed for recoveries.

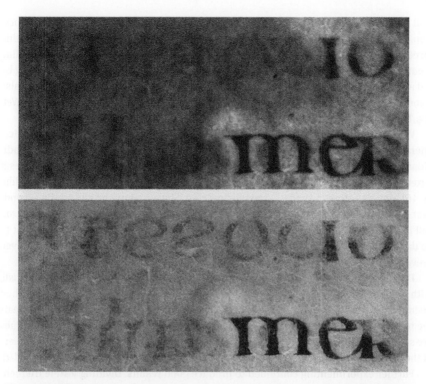

Figure 1.2. Water-damaged text, beginning of first two lines, page 90, St. Chad Gospels. Top: Ultraviolet image, 365 nm. Lower: Merged 638 nm, 535 nm, and 465 nm frequencies. Images reproduced by kind permission of the Chapter of Lichfield Cathedral.

Dividing the RGB multispectral image by nonvisible frequencies, however, proved unsuccessful. Division demonstrates that 850 nm has proportionally similar values for pixels as the RGB image. Once divided, traces of damaged text and bleed-through remain relatively the same (Web Fig. 1.12). At the other end of the spectrum, dividing by 365 nm (ultraviolet) produces likewise disappointing results. Bleed-through still interferes too strongly. However, the damaged text emerges as a bright reddish brown; therefore, finding the appropriate division partner might produce good results (Web Fig. 1.12).

For any recovered text, generating false colour can increase contrast. ImageJ provides a number of luts for doing so. For the damaged text, false colour enhances clarity for dividing by 465 nm, 535 nm, and 638 nm, and some improvement for ultraviolet (Web Fig. 1.13). As mentioned, applying luts requires experimentation. The same lut does not always add clarity to each instance of recovery.

Whether e-Codices or the Digital Walters, because of the large and growing number of available high-resolution images of manuscripts, medievalists have unprecedented opportunities for recovering profound levels of content. This makes splitting RGB images into their red, green, and blue channels a highly significant method. Splitting

RGB images tends not to generate recoveries in their own right. It tends to be the first step. For example, when I split the photograph taken by the British Library, the resulting three channels did not immediately provide results (Web Fig. 1.14). However, dividing them into the colour image does. In all three, bleed-through lessens; in two, dividing by red and blue, recoveries occur: *to* of *tori* and *su* of *suo* (Web Fig. 1.15). Generating false colour enhances these results. For dividing by blue, it leads to recovering *ri* of *tori* (Web Fig. 1.16).

When necessary, results from these recoveries can guide further mathematical operations. For the beginning of page 90, while the results are secure, dividing individual frequencies might produce refined recoveries and provide specific approaches if letters on other pages prove more resistant. Building off good results, such as dividing by 465 nm, therefore, provides a next logical step. Since 638 nm produced the second-best results, I also use this frequency. It provides a nice distance from 465 nm. For iron gall ink, I prefer to divide higher wavelengths by lower ones. This causes parchment to be darker than recoveries. I find bright recoveries more discernible. As a test, however, I reverse them: in case lighter parchment clarifies results.

Dividing frequencies normally produces results in which pages appear blackish, with perhaps faint hints of discernable lines of script. For page 90, this is the case when dividing 638 nm by 465 nm (Web Fig. 1.17). Adjusting the histogram, however, reveals the text. In this case, values for pixels range from about 0 to 3.4804. When these values are stretched to cover the full range (0 to 255), the text emerges (Web Fig. 1.18). A view of the beginning of the first two lines reveals strong recovery (Fig. 1.3 or Web Fig. 1.19).

Further experimenting continued to produce good results. Dividing visible frequencies into each other all generated recoveries. For example, dividing 535 nm by 505 nm and 450 nm by 592 nm provide good views of the damaged text (Web Fig. 1.20). In the second example, to demonstrate recovered text appearing darker, I divide by the higher frequency. Again, lighter text is my preference. However, blemishes or discolouration of parchment can cause one or the other to be more beneficial.

The ultraviolet frequency continued in its trend of not being as beneficial as expected. Dividing each of the other frequencies by 365 nm generates only one image that produces good recoveries: 850 nm by 365 nm (Web Fig. 1.21). This image, however, provides less clarity than those derived from dividing visible frequencies. Results can be unpredictable. Sometimes, the materiality and condition of a manuscript affect reflected light in ways that do not provide the expected leverage. Therefore, guiding principles are important, but they are just that, guidance. For an otherwise overwhelming number of options, they direct and systematize the approach. However, digital recovery requires play and experimentation.

For recovery by division, images produced by a colour camera also provide further opportunities. However, as mentioned, splitting them produces only three images for division, one for each channel: red, green, and blue. Therefore, the possibilities are limited to dividing red by green, red by blue, and green by blue (and the reverse, if preferred). Splitting the photograph taken by the British Library generated solid recovery for the green-channel divided by blue (Web Fig. 1.22). Applying different luts generates false colour, enhancing these results (Web Fig. 1.23).

Figure 1.3. Beginning of first two lines, page 90, St. Chad Gospels. Top: Recoveries from dividing 638 nm by 465 nm. Values stretched across whole histogram. Lower: Overlay of letters to emphasize recovery. Images reproduced by kind permission of the Chapter of Lichfield Cathedral.

Another way to generate false colour and recovery is to merge different frequencies than those expected for an RGB image. For example, a false colour image can be generated by combining green, blue, and ultraviolet frequencies for the red, green, and blue-channels. For page 90, however, merging frequencies in various combinations did not generate beneficial results. Nonetheless, further possibilities exist: the results from divided frequencies can also be merged. For example, merging an infrared frequency for the red-channel, a divided frequency for the green (592 nm divided by 505 nm), and the ultraviolet for the blue produces excellent results (Web Fig. 1.24). The ultraviolet frequency brings more traces of damaged text into the RBG image while infrared fades the bleed-through. However, for the green-channel, dividing the higher frequency by the lower frequency is significant. This causes recovered text to be lighter than its surroundings, generating needed contrast. When the divisor and dividend is reversed, the traces of iron gall ink become darker; however, to my eye, this makes their nuances more difficult to see (Web Fig. 1.24).

Finally, merging channels is not limited to a sole channel containing a divided frequency. Two or all three channels can contain them. In the prior merged image, one of the best divisions for the blue-channel turned out to be 535 nm divided by 465 nm. To find this division, I initially tested results within the general range of the blue-channel and then expanded them. To include a third divided result for the red-channel, I found that 700 nm divided by 625 nm was a good choice (Web Fig. 1.25). Again, enhancing recoveries requires experimentation. Dividing the original RGB image by its three channels provides initial understanding about how bleed-through and damaged text reflects light. From these results, informed experimentation can proceed, increasing the chance of generating revealing results.

Alternative Colour Spaces

Alternative colour spaces provide a substantial number of options for RGB images, whether from a colour or monochrome camera. However, similar to mathematical operations, variations result from a camera's internal software and the sensitivity of a Bayer filter. This can lead to colour spaces providing different levels of recovery. Consequently, as these results demonstrate, it is worth working through the colour models that I recommend (and then trying alternative ones if recoveries are not complete): Lab, YIQ, HSV/HSB, HCY, and CMYK.[26]

Lab provides a promising start because it represents colour through two channels rather than three. This generates opportunities for colour to reveal unseen patterns. For page 90, the b-channel (blue–yellow axis) reveals only some of the damaged text for the 2003 British Library image but all of it for my 2010 image (Web Fig. 1.26). False colour further highlights the recovery (Web Fig. 1.27). In the 2003 image, false colour clarifies damaged letters. While the bleed-through appears as a domineering reddish purple, the damaged text appears as a bright yellow. This heightens parts of letters unobscured by bleed-through, in some instances revealing them better than the false-colour b-channel for the 2010 image, such as the first part of the *u* of *suo*. Therefore, valuable visual information is gained even when only parts of damaged text are revealed.

The a-channel (red–green axis) is similar for both images, suggesting that a variation in chromaticity might provide further results. In the a-channel of Lab, false colour generates good contrast for *illis*, making it visible. However, bleed-through still dominates the first line, limiting recovery for both images (Web Fig. 1.28). Representing colour on a 33-degree rotated axis, YIQ might prove productive. However, its results disappointingly mimic the recovery of Lab. Its I-channel (orange–blue axis) produces good results for the 2010 image whereas recovery for the 2003 image is limited (Web Fig. 1.29). Again, the *u* of *suo* is clearer for the 2003 image. Sometimes, individual or parts of letters are the only results. If this is the case, and only one image is available, recovery depends upon piecing together limited information from various recovery methods. This might not generate the same level of certainty, but it provides information for a good, interpretative case to be made.

Unlike YIQ and Lab, the HSV/HSB colour space produces better results for the 2003 image (Web Fig. 1.30). The beneficial channel is S, providing information for saturation

---

26 For a discussion of further alternative colour spaces, see Duffy, "The Discovery," 2–4.

(the dilution of white). For the 2003 image, *tori su* is discernable in the first line. *Illis* emerges in both images. To try to enhance results, I split the 2003 image into channels using the HSI and LSHLab colour spaces. For both, the S-channel represents saturation. It refines results (Web Fig. 1.31 and Web Fig. 1.32). For false colour, I took a slightly different approach. I applied luts to minimize variations in the parchment and highlight only the traces of damaged letters.

Intriguingly, the HCY colour space reverses the ability of the 2003 and 2010 images to generate recoveries. The C-channel (difference from the nearest grey) generates good results for the 2010 image, with bleed-through dissolving into the parchment. Its results are similar to the 2003 image and the S-channel of HSV/HSB, HSI, and LSHLab. For HCY, the red-coloured bleed-through is dominant in the 2003 image; however, much of the yellow-coloured damaged text is still discernable (Web Fig. 1.33).

The easily overlooked nontristimulus colour model, CMYK, likewise produces positive results. These results occur for the Y-channel (yellow) and are more substantial for the 2003 image (Web Fig. 1.34). While *illis* of the second line is recovered in both, the 2003 image shows better recovery for the first line. Re-examining the colour histograms for both images reveals a larger proportion of yellow in the 2003 image. This likely accounts for the better recovery. The histogram for the 2010 image contains more grey, leaving less yellow to be represented.

Decorrelation Stretch

From both images, decorrelation stretch recovers the damaged text. Like other methods, recovery requires different adjustments. For the 2010 image, choosing YXX in DStretch, the ImageJ plugin, and then the YBK pre-set generates good results (Web Fig. 1.35). However, an advantage of DStretch is making adjustments and watching the changing results. For this, DStretch provides slide-bars for Y, U, and V values (brightness and two chromacity channels). This produces immediate feedback to refine recoveries. By adjusting the Y, U, and V values, I was able to eliminate nearly all of the bleed-through (Web Fig. 1.36 and Web Fig. 1.37).

DStretch confirms what already has been established about the differences in the histograms of the two images. For the 2003 images, choosing YXX and the YBK adjustment produces no recovery. However, manually adjusting Y, U, and V, produces good results (Web Fig. 1.38). When consulting alternative images, different adjustments are required. If digital scans of earlier colour photographs or transparencies are available, supportive and perhaps improved results are possible. The most recent image might not always produce the best recoveries. Recoveries depend also upon how a manuscript has aged.

One final note: DStretch has a smartphone app. It includes pre-sets and adjustable settings, although both are designed for rock art. While not perfect, it generates recoveries for page 90 (Web Fig. 1.39). Its YWE choice recovers *illis* and some of the letters on the first line, and YDT provides an alternative view. However, YYE clarifies damaged letters, with overlay helping to identify them.

Erasures

For the St. Chad Gospels, erasures present stronger challenges for digital recovery than water-damage. The scribes were quite diligent in scraping ink from the parchment, leaving less residue. While erasures present more resistance, various recovery methods produced good results. These recoveries were aided by the design of letters. Letters contain unique combinations of features, making them more readily discernable. Therefore, recovering salient features, even if not a whole letter, can reveal needed clues. Furthermore, errors generally have a logic to them. This information can support recoveries, too. Once identified, digitally overlaying the likely text onto the erased space can test results. These methods made even the longer erasure on page 3 succumb. The erasure on page 141, however, remains mysterious, only partially yielding its secrets.

Erasures, Pages 37 and 78

Upon first examination, the erased letter on page 37 appears unlikely for recovery. Although the RGB image reveals traces, these traces are incongruous with Insular script. They suggest an unrecognizable letter and a *y*, its descender above the baseline. Although faint, however, multiple digital techniques recover this letter: an *m*. The best methods are dividing the RGB image by the 450 nm image, DStretch YXX-YYE, and saturation channel of HSV/HSB (Web Fig. 1.40). Since the 2003 image is missing, I attempted to enhance recovery by using other colour spaces. HSL, which calculates saturation differently from HSV/HSB and HCY, moved recovery in the wrong direction. The best was the saturation channel of LSHLab, previously used to refine recoveries for the S-channel in the 2010 image of page 90. This colour space converts RGB to Lab colour before separating it into channels for lightness, saturation, and hue. The remnants of the *m* are marginally brighter (Web Fig. 1.41).

For this erasure, at the top of the *e*, part of a serif survives. It provides further evidence of an erased *m*. In Insular script, a limited number of letters would leave such remains. The location corresponds with the likes of an Insular *n* or *m*, the serif originally forming part of the lead stem.[27] Although a small space can exist between the top of an *e* and *m*, they regularly touch (Web Fig. 1.42). Of note, to fill the space generated by the erasure, the scribe attempts an artistic flourish. He crafted his scraping to leave ink to form an extended crossbar for the *e* (Web Fig. 1.42). Again, this limits the possible erased letters to those having an initial stroke that could be scraped into such an extended crossbar.

Identifying this erasure as an *m* might seem trivial. However, patterns can emerge from erasures, providing significant evidence. For example, questions exist about how well Insular scribes knew Latin. While once ruled by Rome, England had become dominated by Germanic tribes. Chad, the namesake of the St. Chad Gospels, studied under Aiden, the Irish monk sent from Iona to be abbot of Lindisfarne. For training, Chad also

---

27 Besides an *n* or *m*, such a remnant might also remain from the serif of an *i, g, R, t, u*, or *x*. However, a number of these letters, such as *g* and *x*, would make for an odd Latin word.

travelled to Ireland, like many English monks.[28] Rome never conquered Ireland, so Latin was never a dominant language. Furthermore, the Irish kept their Celtic oral tradition until conversion to Christianity in the fifth and sixth centuries. Consequently, Latin had to be learned, and not from native speakers. For Latin, *m* is a regular ending. If a large number of *ms* are erased, it says something about the state of Latin learning. In the St. Chad Gospels, I have identified features suggesting that at least four scribes copied this great gospel-book.[29] One scribe appears less experienced: his script is less fluent, and he rarely adds flourishes to letters. He would have copied page 37. Because it is common for an *m* to end a word, he might have added one, viewing an ending *e* as incorrect: not knowing the word and its conjugation. Other possibilities likewise exist; however, studying erased letters can lead to patterns emerging that contribute to overall understanding and perhaps evidence from which to generate or support insights into scribal practices and learning.

Similarly, digital methods generated good recovery for the erased letters on page 78. For recovery, I had images from 2003 and 2010. Both produced good results. However, when consulting either of these images, this recovery is fairly certain: an erased *ni* and possibly an erased unidentifiable letter and *b*, the latter two turning out to be ink transfer (Web Fig. 1.43). This erasure occurs in the second sentence of Matthew 17:19. Before erased, the clause begins *nisi* (unless) and is erased to begin *si* (if). *Si* is the expected word for the Vulgate. The St. Chad Gospels is predominantly a Vulgate version of the gospels. However, after Jerome completed his Vulgate version, Old Latin variants re-entered the text. These variants survived in Old Latin copies of the gospels and the writings of the early Church Fathers, who quoted these earlier versions of the gospels. People corrected their Vulgate to return it to preferred wording and phrasing. These variations entered into exemplars and show relations among monasteries and their gospels.[30] For this erasure, *nisi* appears in Old Latin texts, and significantly in the Hereford Gospels (Hereford Cathedral Library, MS P.I.2). The text of the Hereford Gospels most nearly matches that of the St. Chad Gospels, sharing 774 recensions.[31] Therefore, this erasure likely occurred later, perhaps in the twelfth or thirteenth century, when punctuation was likewise altered and added.

In colour images of page 78, bleed-through appears as if written on two slightly different lines. This suggests erasure or transferred ink (Web Fig. 1.44). To account for bleed-through, I overlaid text from the opposite side of the page, page 77. The potentially erased *b* still appears. But when I overlaid text that would transfer from the opposite page, page 79, the potentially erased *b* disappears: a horizontally reversed *d* overlays it. In the colour image, while difficult to discern, the bowl of this potentially erased *b*

---

28 Bede, *The Ecclesiastical History*, 164, 178.

29 Endres, "The St. Chad Gospels: Ligatures," 164–86.

30 A genealogy of recensions shows families of Italian texts as sources for Insular gospels. See Fischer, *Lateinische Bibelhandschriften*; McNamara, "Irish Gospel Texts"; Burton, *The Old Latin Gospels*.

31 Hopkins-James, *The Celtic Gospels*, xil.

does not curve into its ascender like a normal Insular *b*. Instead, as an Insular *d*, it has a straight stem. This is readily viewable in the overlay. Because the St. Chad Gospels experienced water-damage, ink transfer is a common but intermittent complication. Ruling out this transfer verifies this erasure as *ni* (Web Fig. 1.44).

Erasure on Page 3

The erasure on page 3 appears challenging. It is nearly the whole line, providing the scribe ample space to scrape rigorously with his knife. Furthermore, as with the erasure on page 78, it is complicated by bleed-through and ink transferred (Web Fig. 1.45 and Web Fig. 1.46). The transfer is extensive and likely interferes with sorting out the upper portion of letters, their traces already obscured by substantial bleed-through. Transferred ink tends to be more difficult. In minimizing bleed-through, digital recovery benefits from parchment affecting reflected light before it reaches the ink on the opposite side. Transferred ink resides on the same side. And unlike a palimpsest, its composition is the same as the traces of ink for damaged text.

Still, I was able to recover this text. My digital methods, however, were aided by two factors. First, letters are composed of unique combinations of features, features designed to make them easily identified for reading. It is paramount for readers to assemble letters rapidly into words and words into phrases and sentences for meaning. Unique combinations of features also benefit recovery. For example, to begin recovery, examining the erased area on a high-resolution RBG image reveals the last erased letter as a *t*. The scribe likely did not want to scrape too rigorously near the *et* symbol, which begins the correctly copied text. The visible features of this Insular *t* include remnants of its upper cross-stroke, the curve of its stem as it forms its lower portion, and its ending serif, a unique set of distinguishing features. Also, searching this line for remnants, toward the middle, I find a trace of ink from what appears to be a serif, located between the two stems of an *N* that bleeds through (Web Fig. 1.47). This serif presents a good target to begin digital recovery.

Attempting various methods, I found that dividing 730 nm by 365 nm, then generating false colour, produced the most vivid results for this serif (Web Fig. 1.47). It shows a stem that curves toward the bottom of the letter. Such a curve constructs multiple letters, such as *a*, *b*, *c*, *d*, *e*, *o*, or *u*. However, the serif terminating this stem at the mid-height of a line means that it can only represent one possible letter: *u*. Therefore, I know that this line originally had a *u* at this point.

Other recovery methods produced results for other letters. However, dividing 535 nm by 465 nm and 592 nm by 505 nm and combining the results with 940 nm produced an RGB image that reveals multiple letters. At the beginning of the erasure, it reveals an *I*, which for Insular scribes also represents a *J*. About three-fourth of the way into the erasure, it reveals the loop of a letter below the baseline. The only Insular letter possessing such a loop is a *g*. Finally, at the end, it reveals *ui*, just prior to the *t* (Fig. 1.4 or Web Fig. 1.48). When informed by the content of surrounding verses, these recoveries provide enough information to propose a critically reasoned possibility: "Iechoniam autem genuit."

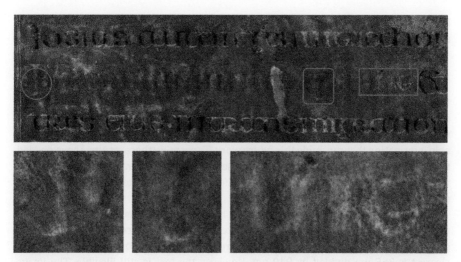

Figure 1.4. Top: Erased text, line 13, page 3, St. Chad Gospels. 535 nm divided by 465 nm, 592 nm divided by 505 nm, and 940 nm merged into RGB image. Lower left: Recovered *I* or Insular *J* (inside circle). Lower center: Recovered loop of letter (inside rounded square), distinguishing feature of Insular *g*. Lower right: Recovered *uit.* Images reproduced by kind permission of the Chapter of Lichfield Cathedral.

For proposing this possibility, knowing the content of the gospels is key. The erasure occurs in the opening of the gospel of Matthew, as he narrates the genealogy of Jesus. The narrative has a rhythm: someone *autem genuit* (and begot) someone, and that someone begot someone else. Intermittently, Matthew provides additional information, breaking the rhythm. The erasure begins at a point where the rhythm is broken. Trusting this rhythm, the scribe likely copied, "Iechoniam autem genuit," following the previous line, "Joseas autem genuit Iechoniam" (Matthew 1:11–12). However, at this point, the gospel text breaks its rhythm with "et fratres eius in transmigratione Babyloins." When I test this recovery by copying these words from elsewhere on the page, I find that they perfectly fit the space (Web Fig. 1.49). Furthermore, when I overlay the text onto the most consistent recovery method for the erasure, I find traces of other letters, such as the *e*, *c*, *h*, *o*, *n*, *i*, *a*, and *m* of *Iechoniam* (Web Fig. 1.50), and the *a* and *t* of *autem*. If I overlay bleed-through and transferred ink, recovered traces appear in areas left unscathed by obscuring effects (Web Fig. 1.51).

From erasures, whole letters might not be recoverable. However, distinguishing features, such as the loop of a *g*, can reveal needed information to identify them. Combining information from digital recoveries with knowledge of the content can lead to proposing critically reasoned possibilities. Through overlay, these possibilities can be tested, the overlaid letters, when possible, taken from the same page, assuring the scribal hand and characteristics of the day's work. Visual information from such overlays can be augmented by overlaying bleed-through and transferred ink, further assuring results. Regularly, these additional overlays make evident further traces of digitally recovered letters. But finally, and importantly, with all recoveries, confirm them by consulting high-resolution colour images, and when possible, the manuscript.

Page 141

I exhausted the methods available to me and could not recover all of the erased content on page 141. In the future, employing other digital imaging methods, such as X-ray or ultraviolet fluorescence, might garner results. However, my methods did produce valuable information that can guide this future work. To examine these results, I have divided this erasure into two parts. I begin with the right-hand side, which appears to have writing under the *in* of the second *finit* on the line, writing in the middle, and imagery along the border on the right.

The writing in the middle appears as if it is recoverable. In colour images, it is fairly visible (Web Fig. 1.52). However, division, alternative colour spaces, DStretch, and merging alternative images for RGB channels produced unsatisfactory results. One of the clearest is 365 nm divided by 940 nm. However, the text is still illegible. The image shows an intriguing light squiggly line. This suggests that features of the parchment might be inferring with recovery and what is seen. As I experimented with various digital approaches, dividing the RGB image by 365 nm produces what appears to be a view of the parchment without remnants of text. The squiggly line remains clear, but the image reveals features of the parchment that might also be interfering with what is visible. These features include impressions left in the parchment, perhaps by letters (Web Fig. 1.53). In the next chapter, I will examine these surface details with RTI.

The right side of this erasure, however, is a different story. Viewable in colour images, the imagery along the border appears to be a bird, perhaps feeding hatchlings in a nest. It is visible through a range of recovery approaches, including the 940 nm infrared image; merging 365 nm, 592 nm, and 940 nm divided by 365 nm; Q-channel of YIQ colour space; and DStretch YXX (Web Fig. 1.54). All four also show other lines, perhaps an interlace pattern. The merged channels and DStretch provide the clearest view of these lines. Because this bird is so near the decoration of the border, the scribe might have erased it less rigorously. This bird opens the possibility that a majority of this erased content might be imagery, not text.

The text below the *in* of *finit* appears to be an *H* with a partial circle around it. But like attempts to recover other text for this erasure, digital methods left it riddled. Merged 465 nm, 535 nm, and 940 nm divided by 850 nm provides one of the clearest results (Web Fig. 1.55). But this view still does not clarify the text. Curiously, 365 nm divided by 940 nm reveals text below the first part of the *F*, text otherwise obscured by a dark area of parchment. This area provides a good target for future imaging. The RGB image divided by 365 nm reveals a lightened area for these letters (Web Fig. 1.56). But alas, none of the images reveal enough details to make the text legible.

The second part, space further toward the left margin, reveals what seems to be more imagery. Below the second *i* of the first *finit*, a finger appears. It is recovered by various methods (Web Fig. 1.57). However, the area below it is unclear. It might be the remainder of a hand, but digital methods did not clarify it. Intriguingly, the S-channel of the HSV/HSB colour space and Q-channel of the YIQ colour space reveal what appears to be a second finger further toward the left margin. However, this is likely an illusion caused by discolouration and scrapes from the erasure. The area that appears as if a rendered fingernail is darkened parchment, perhaps dirt (Web Fig. 1.58).

While recovery methods did not reveal any text, recognizing that this erasure contains imagery is an important discovery. The date of the imagery, however, is difficult to know. The St. Chad Gospels does not contain other pointing fingers,[32] and the style of the bird does not match other birds. Also, how scribes and artists handle the last page of a gospel is uncertain. For the gospels of Luke and John, the last page does not survive. The other last page to survive is Mark's. It is unframed, but it contains an extra version of the Lord's Prayer, likely for swearing oaths.[33] Accompanying the Lord's Prayer is decoration, a large interlace star flowing out of the opening *P* of *Pater*. The same style of this star occurs on other pages, such as page 7, where it likely represents the star of Bethlehem. Although the imagery raises as many questions as it answers, it opens possibilities and provides information for further exploration. Hopefully, future imaging can unravel this mystery.

Recovering Pigments

When faced with a severely damaged page, such as the incipit of Matthew (page 1), recovery is limited. For years, as mentioned, this incipit likely served as the outer protection for the manuscript. Its intricate beasts, interlace, and serpents have been worn to shadows. However, alternative colour spaces and false colour can help to reveal pigments and create contrast significant for understanding these creatures and their visual impact on meaning. For this task, DStretch functions exceptionally well. It efficiently generates contrast and amplifies damaged pigments, especially reds, greens, and yellows. For page 1, applying the CRGB pre-set reveals an enhanced sense of this page's one-time dynamic interplay of beasts, serpents, interlace, and text (Web Fig. 1.59).

Because pigments are severely damaged, recovery methods can invigorate them and their images. This is significant because such images were originally vivid and central to meaning. For example, DStretch highlights a coiled serpent biting a strand of interlace (Web Fig. 1.60). While wear has muted its colour, this serpent originally was a lush, dark green, likely the pigment verdigris, found on the portrait of Luke.[34] Similar to the portrait of Luke, artists contrasted this green with a brownish-red pigment, likely the lichen

---

32 Pointing fingers or hands (*maniculae*) are a common feature of later medieval manuscripts (Kwakkel, "Filling a Void," 21–22). But they also appear in Insular manuscripts, such as on folios 4r and 30r of the ninth-century Macregol Gospels (Bodleian Library, MS Auct. C. 2. 19). However, dating them is always difficult. In the Macregol Gospels, however, their style and ink echo the script.

33 Brown, "Lichfield/Llandeilo Gospels," 59.

34 The bluish nature of what remains of this pigment might likewise suggest that it is vergaut, a green pigment generated by mixing orpiment with indigo.

orchil or orcein, generating eye-catching effects.[35] The serpent appears in the upper portion of the *I* of *Liber* (the first word of the gospel). The *I* intersects the horizontal line of the *L*, forming a cross. Facilitating this cross, the *L* is smaller and placed in the upper half of the page, whereas the *I* runs its full length. Another coiled green serpent mirrors the upper one, directly below it. A similar pair of white serpents extend horizontally, between the two green ones. Together, they form a cross of serpents, a second cross at the point where the *L* and *I* intersect.

Matching the lush green of the serpents, verdigris likewise colours the bodies of beasts that construct borders for three lines of smaller script. This script presents the next five words of Matthew's gospel. Through colour, the serpents are connected to these words, perhaps referencing Matthew 10:16, in which Jesus instructs his apostles about going out into the world and preaching the gospels: "Behold, I send you as sheep in the middle of wolves. Therefore, be wise as serpents." The bodies of beasts surrounding the words of God echo the circumstance of sheep in the middle of wolves. The serpents provide a reminder to be wise—but also likely an assurance of rebirth into the eternal, another feature of Christianity, symbolized by serpents shedding their skin.[36] Combined with the double-cross, such references prime Christians for entering Matthew's gospels. This opening visual wonder and its meaning exemplifies what makes the St. Chad Gospels such an artistic achievement.

Methods are also valuable for recovering pigment on less damaged pages. In the St. Chad Gospels, the pigment that has suffered most is orpiment. I attempted to recover it on two less damaged pages, the portrait and incipit of Mark (Web Fig. 1.61). The extent of its loss is not easily observed. I experimented with a number of colour spaces and false colours, attempting to increase its contrast and amplify any muted traces of its yellow. The |3-channel of the |1|2|3 colour model allows false colour to simplify the range of colours and generate contrast for remnants of orpiment (Web Fig. 1.62). However, I found the efficiency of DStretch made the work easier and more productive (Web Fig. 1.63). For example, DStretch recovers and highlights orpiment that once decorated the borders of Mark's robe. Against the varying brownish reds of the robe, the yellow borders would have been stunning. A magnified view reveals the small, trace amounts of orpiment that remain and the power of digital methods to reveal them (Web Fig. 1.64).

Concluding Comments

For recovering damaged content, prospects have never been better. Advances in noninvasive digital methods continue to build upon previous methods and results, demonstrating the advantages of approaching recoveries through the physics of light. Accelerating this

---

35 This reddish-brown pigment, which takes on all sorts of variations, has previously been identified as folium. However, recent studies suggest it is orchil or orcein (Brown, *The Lindisfarne*, 281; Meehan, *The Book of Kells*, 224–25).

36 For the serpent representing rebirth and two additional Christian attributes, see Curley, *Physiologus*, 16–19.

development, methods of image analysis stretch across disciplines. From astrophysics to medical imaging, a variety of disciplines are developing and refining software and making it available. The open-source and open-architecture of ImageJ represents a stellar example. Not only does it and its rapidly developed plugins benefit its intended users in medicine, but it also benefits those working with geographic surveys, rock art, and manuscripts. The physics of light knows no disciplinary boundary. But as significantly, more and more libraries, museums, and archives are placing high-resolution images of their manuscripts online, many with options to download. Medievalists, therefore, are well positioned to recover vast amounts of lost content, propelling scholarship forward in exciting ways.

The opportunities opened by digital imaging, however, are only beginning. Various techniques, whether high-resolution colour, MSI, or HSI, provide breathtaking opportunities. Although high-resolution colour cameras provide substantial data for recoveries, techniques such as MSI and HSI provide added prospects. By capturing information about how a manuscript reflects nonvisible light and different wavelengths, they allow unseen patterns to emerge. However, these advanced techniques regularly require post-processing. For this, effective methods are available, such as mathematical operations, combining alternative frequencies into an RGB image, and alternative colour spaces. If only colour images exist, options include splitting RGB images into their three channels (then, applying mathematical operations) and using alternative colour spaces. After any of these methods, false colour can be applied to generate greater contrast. These advances represent the second wave of digital contribution, recoveries that can occur even from images taken with a smartphone.[37] By understanding the properties of light and learning recovery methods, medievalists position themselves to make countless contributions, solving mysteries concealed on damaged pages, conveyed in riddled light.

Note

* All Web Figures referred to in this chapter can be accessed at billendres.com/book/chap1/chap1.html.

---

37 As mentioned, many libraries and archives allow photographs taken with a smartphone. This makes data available for digital recovery. However, using an app that captures data in a raw format provides more data for digital recovery. Other formats, such as JPEGs, lose visual information during compression.

Chapter 2

REFLECTANCE TRANSFORMATION IMAGING: AN ENHANCED VIEW OF SURFACE DETAILS*

IF NORMAL DIGITIZATION has an alter ego, it is reflectance transformation imaging (RTI). Digitization generally treats all surface details as equal in the eyes of lighting. If shadows occur, they are removed, using techniques such as flat-field correction.[1] This, in effect, turns a page into a flat surface. By contrast, RTI celebrates a page as a play of light. It revels in how each detail participates, capturing these dynamics for pigment, parchment, and ink. For example, as discussed in Chapter 1, recovering the yellow pigment orpiment is important because it emulates divine wisdom, its light pouring forth from the page. To make the effect of light more dynamic, artists layered pigments, generating textured swells of colour that increase the complexity of reflected light. For the later Book of Kells, Bernard Meehan has speculated that such layering had a further aim: through aging, cracking, and chipping, layered pigments would generate an evolving and enriched interplay of colour and light.[2] For an illuminated manuscript such as the St. Chad Gospels, this interplay is an essential part of religious expression. Unfortunately, normal digitization fails to capture its dynamics.

By removing shadow, digitization not only diminishes the visual experience of a page, but it also conceals material details. As mentioned, multiple scholars critique interpretation that overlooks the contributions of materiality to meaning. In the example of the portrait of Mark, the shimmer of orpiment is echoed in how the artist portrays him, stepping onto the decorative border, the threshold of the page. It implies that Mark is stepping into the world, opening a path from the sacred and into the physical. To miss the material effect of orpiment is to miss its echoing of Mark's gesture, an emphasis that provides a cosmological orientation for entering the gospels. Such use of materiality is central to complex artistic expression, its triumph perhaps best expressed by the twelfth-century Welshman Giraldus Cambrensis. Upon seeing an early Irish gospelbook, he exclaims that it "must have been the result of work, not of men, but of angels."[3] Contemplating the rich history of such artistic expression, the twentieth-century philosopher Hans-Georg Gadamer concludes that aesthetic experience is the epistemic contribution of the humanities.[4] By stifling the experience of materiality, normal digitization limits access to humanistic epistemic content.

---

1 Flat-fielding mathematically normalizes brightness, correcting it for pixels in which the lighting or sensitivity of photodetectors varies.

2 Meehan, *The Book of Kells*, 228.

3 Cambrensis, *The History and Topography*, 84.

4 Gadamer, *Truth and Method*. For Gadamer, every structure of thought must be understood as an element within its total context, which is expressed through an aesthetics. See particularly Chapter 3.

In the earthly realm of scholarship, however, a shadowless image limits access to significant details, thus information. These details provide crucial evidence about manuscripts, such as hair follicles and impressions from rulings to understand relations to other manuscripts. But also highly telling evidence goes uncaptured, such as dry-point writing. A prime motive for my pursuit of RTI is dry-point. Etched with a stylus but no ink, dry-point is meant to go unseen.[5] It is notoriously difficult to discern. When discussing it, scholars regularly qualify their readings. One reason for this is that when raking light follows the direction of a scratched line, it disappears. Providing control over lighting, RTI eliminates this problem. It requires a series of photographs taken from the same position but with different directional lighting. Its software combines these images into a single file, which when observed, allows control over lighting and mathematical enhancements for amplifying surface details (Web Fig. 2.1). When viewing an RTI file, a scholar, therefore, can adjust directional lighting until it strikes any part of a dry-point letter at a favourable angle to expose it.

In this chapter, I explore RTI and its ability to capture surface details. Such capture increases digital access to the materiality of a manuscript, including rulings, hair follicles, and dry-point writing. In addition, it exposes rising inks and pigments, providing visual information about risks and areas needing special care. Essential to this chapter, however, is my work with RTI and dry-point writing in the St. Chad Gospels. Through it, I reveal the technique's unparalleled ability to capture dry-point, an ability that can transform its study. Dry-point has lacked sufficient study because it is notoriously difficult to see, let alone photograph, limiting scholarly dialogue and debate about it. While control over the direction of lighting provides a substantial gain, RTI increases this benefit through mathematical enhancements such as diffuse gain, specular enhancement, and normals visualizations. These enhancements prove invaluable for discerning dry-point, but they also assist in recovering information about damaged or erased content. RTI also benefits from having two different free viewers available (with differing features) and two types of processed files (providing different mathematical enhancements). Finally, I argue that light is as much a part of the artistic palette as pigment, ink, and parchment, a casualty in regular digitization but one returned to scholars through RTI.

Decisions and Methods

Initially, RTI relied on a dome. This restricted its use for manuscripts. The technique was developed in 2001 by Tom Malzbender and Dan Gelb at Hewlett-Packard Laboratories. They originally named it polynomial texture mapping (PTM), the name deriving from Malzbender and Gelb reconstructing the surface colour of a pixel when the angle of lighting changed through biquadratic polynomial coefficients.[6] Because these calculations require a static camera position and known angles for the sources of lighting, they used a dome. It provided a stationary location for a camera and known locations for the lighting for its angles to a photographed subject. Also, each source

---

5 Dry-point is also referred to as "hardpoint" or "metalpoint."
6 Malzbender et al., "Polynomial Texture Maps," 519–20.

of lighting needed to emit the same energy, and a dome maintained an equal distance between each source and a photographed object. Finally, a dome blocked peripheral, polluting sources of lighting that could interfere with results. A dome, therefore, provided the perfect solution.

For manuscripts, however, a dome presents difficulties. To block outside lighting, early domes had bottoms, which necessitated a door to place objects inside. These doors tended to be small, restricted by wiring and lighting. Manuscripts regularly were larger. Furthermore, staging a page inside a dome is challenging. Parchment can be rigid. Bindings exacerbate the problem. Coaxing a page into a level position and managing the rise of the opposite side requires space to work, difficult or impossible to accomplish inside a dome. This necessitates a bottomless dome, one that can be raised for setup and lowered over a manuscript for imaging. Finally, building a dome is costly, and transporting it is cumbersome. These restrictions led to a clever solution: calculate the direction of lighting from its reflection on a ball, placed inside the frame of each photograph. This approach is known as highlight RTI. For brevity, I will refer to it simply as RTI, unless I need to make a distinction. Without requiring a dome, RTI becomes viable for manuscripts.

As the positioning of lighting changes, however, highlight RTI still requires keeping it an equal distance from the subject. A simple solution was found: a piece of string. Although I have experimented with technological solutions (such as laser measuring tools), string remains best. Cut to the needed length (three to four times the length of a page), it provides an easy and cost-efficient solution, one with minimal risk to a manuscript. String and reflecting ball make possible the use of hand-held lighting sources, rendering RTI highly portable. No longer restricted by the dimensions of a dome and highly portable, RTI is available and irreplaceable for studying manuscripts.

For good results, RTI must account for three crucial elements: the number of photographs needed, direction of lighting needed for each photograph, and a strategy for eliminating the contaminating effects of peripheral light. Generally, RTI requires 24 to 60 photographs. However, I have tested and achieved beneficial results with 20. Smaller numbers of photographs are necessary when a tight binding causes a manuscript to open to less than 150 degrees, requiring the opposite pages to be staged at an upward slant (Web Fig. 2.2). In such cases, photographs taken with lighting at lower angles will not be possible from the raised side. Yet, such conditions do not prevent benefits.

During RTI, guidance is helpful for positioning the handheld flash. This can be provided by the tripod, part of the portable RTI equipment. A tripod generally supplies the static position for the camera. I find that roughly forty-five photographs produce excellent results, generating flexibility if anomalies occur, such as technical glitches or me getting my hand in one of the photographs.[7] Forty-five divides evenly by three, resulting in fifteen photographs taken within each of the three openings between the legs of a tripod. The triangular openings furthermore make for a nice, simple pattern, beginning

---

7 For my approach, I am grateful to the West Semitic Research Project, directed by Bruce Zuckerman. In 2014, I received a grant from them for training and the loan of an RTI kit for my project.

Figure 2.1. Left: Setup for RTI. Hereford Gospels, Hereford Cathedral Library, Hereford, England. Photo: Gordon Taylor LRPS © Hereford Cathedral, 2016. Right: Pattern for positions of lighting between two of the legs of the tripod to generate fifteen of the forty-five photographs for an RTI file.

with the flash held for the first photograph at the top, then moving downward, a row of two, three, four, and five. For each row, the flash is evenly spaced from top to bottom and side to side. For the bottom row, the flash is held at approximate a 15-degree angle to the page (Fig. 2.1 or Web Fig. 2.3). Lesser angles prove unbeneficial. To maintain the distance of the lighting from the page, a pre-cut piece of string, tied to the end of the flash, makes for a quick measurement. Although I have experimented with different patterns, this one produces excellent results, and its simplicity leads to fewer errors during a long day of imaging.

To eliminate the contaminating effects of peripheral light requires a balancing act. Total darkness is not necessary, but the ability to have dim lighting is beneficial. The balancing act occurs among three camera settings: ISO,[8] shutter speed, and aperture. For shutter speed, I generally prefer 1/125 or 1/200. This is a quick speed and eliminates risks of a long, open shutter. It also eliminates much peripheral light. ISO controls the light sensitivity of the sensor. As it increases, image noise also increases. I generally prefer ISO

---

8 ISO stands for the International Organization of Standardization, the body that sets ratings for the sensitivity of sensors in cameras.

set at 100 or 200. Aperture controls the size of the opening of the shutter. Measured in f-stops, lower numbers represent wider openings. Complicating this choice, the f-stop also changes the depth of field, the distance behind the point of focus that remains in focus. As f-stop increases, so too does the depth of field, with less light entering the camera. Generally, I set f-stop between 7 and 11. Therefore, the balancing act requires not introducing noise from too large of an ISO and having a substantial enough f-stop to produce a depth of field for a page of parchment that might have layered pigment and some cockling. For a dimly lit room, the above range of settings generally provide plenty of flexibility for this balance. When this balance is met, it produces a digital photograph with values for its pixels from zero to low single digits, signaling that the handheld flash is providing the light for the details and shadows captured.[9]

Further flexibility is also available through the settings on the flash. Based on the ISO, f-stop, and shutter speed, the brightness of the flash can be increased or decreased. Therefore, a good quality flash is important, one that adjusts easily and can be hand-held and triggered through a transmitter that slips onto the hot shoe of the camera. When photographing a manuscript, a concern is always damage caused by lighting. This damage is generally produced by ultraviolet light. Because of wedding photography, pro-fessional quality flashes, as well as flashes in general, do not emit ultraviolet light. When photographing a wedding dress, ultraviolet produces a blue hue, ruining the photograph. Therefore, flashes are manufactured to eliminate frequencies in this range.

For RTI, equipment is significant but varies. For the St. Chad Gospels, I used a 22-megapixel DSLR (Digital Single Lens Reflex Camera). Recently, I switched to a 50-megapixel camera, although this decision was prompted by other digital work. A 50-megapixel sensor provides brilliant detail; however, I can always reduce image size if I desire. For lenses, I carry 50 mm and 100 mm macro lenses, 30 mm wide-angle lens,[10] and 24–105 mm telephoto lens. For lenses, flexibility is important. Manuscripts vary greatly in size, from pocket gospel-books to deluxe illuminated manuscripts. Because RTI captures surface details, macro lenses are beneficial, having shorter focal distances than regular lenses.[11] Also, professional grade lenses are crucial. First, they generate the sharpest images. Second, they are well built. I cannot overemphasize the need for well-built lenses. Because shooting generally occurs with the lens pointing downward, the lens needs a tight, well-constructed focusing ring. Each time a DSLR takes a pho-tograph, the mirror lifts to expose the sensor to entering light. Once the mirror lifts, it drops back into place making a click sound. This generates a slight vibration. In a poorly constructed lens, during a sequence of forty-five images, this vibration can cause the lens to drift downward, generating images that grow slightly larger. Because RTI is

---

9 Lenses are highly significant. I use professional macro lenses. However, a smaller f-stop does not interfere with RTI as it does with normal macro photography, which emphasizes details of its close-up view of a subject by allowing all else to shift into a blurred state.

10 For wide angle, I would have chosen a macro lens, but the macro lens made by the manufacturer of my camera did not perform well with my camera's sensor.

11 For a discussion of macro photography for RTI, see Cosentino, "Macro Photography."

dependent upon exactly aligned (registered) images, any lens drift ruins the final RTI file (Web Fig. 2.4).[12]

One of the most significant pieces of equipment is the tripod. It needs to be high-quality and lightweight. Having high-quality leg-locking is imperative. Any shift in the tripod during a forty-five-image sequence causes image misalignment. For travel, lite-weight is essential. Furthermore, a tripod for which the leg angle has at least two settings generates flexibility. This allows a wider spread between the legs. If there is restricted ceiling space or a large manuscript, having the option to spread the legs can make the difference between imaging or not.

But as with all photography, success depends on the time-consuming part: staging. Staging a page can be exasperating. Parchment has a mind of its own, and a tight binding increases its obstinacy. To produce good results, the plane of the lens needs to be parallel to the page. Otherwise, the resulting image will have a distorted perspective. Coaxing a page to lie flat regularly involves elevating a corner or side of the manuscript. Massaging a binding only helps so much. Book snakes can be useful for the opposite side, but when placed on a page, they cast a shadow. For adjustments, having ready materials is essential. Two materials that provide flexibility and work well are poker chips and playing cards. Poker chips interlock, supplying stability if a page needs to be raised. Playing cards enable minor adjustments. For imaging, I place a manuscript on foam book supports covered with a black cloth; any adjusting material can be concealed beneath the cloth. For placing the ruler and reflective balls within the frame of the photograph, a handy tool designed for welding and soldering performs well: helping hands. Helping hands have two arms with clamps at the ends; they are infinitely adjustable. They enable adjusting the height of the balls and ruler to that of the page. This is essential because everything needs to be on the same plane for imaging.

When processing the forty-five images into a single file, I process them into PTM files. This adds flexibility. For highlight RTI, images have two possible file types: PTM and RTI. Both can produce specular mathematical enhancements and a normals visualization. Specular enhancement intensifies reflective qualities, thereby heightening the view of surface details. A normals visualization is a false-colour rendering that shows the direction at which light reflects for each pixel, represented as red, green, and blue. This false-colour reveals the contours of the surface. PTM files, however, provide additional mathematical enhancement, generating significant advantages. These mathematical enhancements include the likes of diffuse gain, which takes features that show rapid changes in height or depth and amplifies them. Such options add flexibility and prove beneficial when sorting out small details, such as the roughly scratched lines of dry-point letters. Nevertheless, RTI files tend to distribute lighting more evenly. This can mitigate

---

12 On my second day of imaging in the library at Lichfield Cathedral, I experienced this problem with professional-grade lenses. However, its cause was fire inspectors walking around the library, located on the second floor of the thirteenth-century cathedral. They generated enough vibration to cause the lens to drift downward. This was unexpected. My first day of imaging had produced spectacular results.

jumps in shadows when viewing a file generated from a reduced number of photographs, caused by such issues as a tight binding limiting the number of photographs taken. Also, RTI files tend to be brighter (Web Fig. 2.5). But choosing between these two file types is not an either/or: photographs can be reprocessed as many times as desired, generating both types of files. To generate PTM and RTI files, free software is available: the RTIBuilder, developed by Cultural Heritage Imaging (CHI) and Universidade do Minho.[13] It includes a PTM fitter (PTM files) and an HSH fitter (RTI files).

Once files are generated, two free RTI viewers are also available, each with advantages: InscriptiFact, developed by the West Semitic Research Project (WSRP), and RTI Viewer, developed by CHI (Web Fig. 2.6).[14] The RTI Viewer functions well for demonstrations and generates snapshots for areas of interest. In demonstrations, it is easy to use and provides the audience with an intuitive ball for apprehending adjustments made to directional lighting. Also, it provides a bookmark setting for easy and quick jumps to desired views. To generate a snapshot, the RTI viewer captures the area framed in the viewer, at its highest resolution. With the snapshot, it generates an XML file, providing information about lighting position, panning, and values of mathematical enhancements.

For study, however, InscriptiFact affords two major advantages. First, it provides an adjustment for luminance. This adjustment is crucial when attempting a recovery when an acute angle of lighting reveals hints of content, yet the whole area is dark. Increasing luminance can lift subtle recoveries out of the darkness. Second, when InscriptiFact generates a snapshot, it is rendered at the highest resolution for the whole page. When viewing it later, this benefits discoveries for other surface details not initially examined that respond to similar lighting and mathematical enhancements.

Both viewers provide one further benefit worth mentioning. It echoes my discussion in the first chapter about testing recoveries against high-resolution colour image and, when possible, against the manuscript. When applying a specular enhancement, both viewers provide control over colour. Through a slide-bar, colour can be eliminated, generating better contrast. However, colour can also be reintroduced, helpful to confirm discoveries by checking for anomalies generated by a greyscale view.

When approaching RTI, having two options for viewers and two options for file types provides flexibility. As I work, I test discoveries among these options. Testing results in this manner is important. Scholars must attempt to critically assess any discovery that relies on algorithms and mathematical enhancements. And although RTI does not have a ready peer for capturing surface details, discoveries should likewise be tested against the results from other advanced imaging techniques, and whenever possible, by consulting the source of the details: the manuscript.

---

13 To download the RTIBuilder, visit CHI: http://culturalheritageimaging.org. For RTIBuilder, CHI provides downloadable instructions.

14 At the time of this writing, available for download were InscriptiFact (version 10.0, build 286, 2017): http://inscriptifact.com/; and RTI Viewer (version 1.1, 2013): http://culturalheritageimaging.org. Both provide downloadable instructions.

Results and Discussion

RTI proved successful in capturing a variety of surface details, including rulings, scrapings, hair follicles, and rising pigments and inks. It also grants a view of pages in shifting light, a facet of their artistic expression and meaning. However, significant to my primary concern, RTI impressively captures dry-point writing. Through its results, I confirmed or refined readings for dry-point on pages identified as having it. For example, on page 221, I was able to discern two previously unnoticed diminutive letters, etched into a narrowing space, restricted by decoration. Additionally, on this page, I discovered new dry-point in the middle of the bottom margin and two others, one above and one below a beast that resides on the left-hand side of the page.

For discovering and discerning dry-point, two mathematical enhancements proved highly beneficial: specular enhancement and diffuse gain. As mentioned, specular enhancement intensifies reflective qualities, and diffuse gain takes features that show rapid changes in height or depth and amplifies them. Using specular enhancement, I confirmed the three names of Anglo-Saxon men on page 217, *Wulfun*, *Alchelm*, and *Eadrit*, and the three names of Anglo-Saxon women on page 226, *Berhtfled*, *Elfled*, and *Wulfild* (Fig. 2.2 or Web Fig. 2.7).[15, 16] Verifying the names of the first two Anglo-Saxon women, however, proved more difficult. They live up to the reputation of dry-point as notoriously difficult to discern. Even in raking light and magnified, the first name, *Berhtfled*, is challenging to detect (Web Fig. 2.8). When applying diffuse gain and specular enhancement, it becomes more discernible (Web Fig. 2.9). Changing the raking lighting to the left-hand side clarifies letters (Web Fig. 2.10). For viewing dry-point, control over lighting is irreplaceable. As necessary for *Berhtfled*, this control affords the ability to change the directional lighting for each letter, illuminating the etched lines as light comes into a perpendicular angle to them, making a letter legible.

A difficulty in interpreting dry-point is that letters can change when directional lighting changes. My discovery of two additional letters on page 221 provides a good example. In the middle of the left-hand margin, scholars had identified the dry-point as *Dulf*.[17] However, RTI enables viewing a descender on the stem of the *D*, allowing its identification as a *P*, an Anglo-Saxon wynn or modern-day *W* (Web Fig. 2.11). The first part of the word, therefore, is *Wulf*. RTI also reveals two further etched letters. Because of their diminished size, these letters went unobserved. The scribe had reduced them to fit into the narrowing space above the curved body of a beast and below the decorative border of the *q* of *quoniam*. These etched letters are *UN*. But identifying them depends upon the

---

15 Charles-Edwards and McKee, "Lost Voices," 81–82.

16 These three female names appear on the page with the *Magnificat*, Mary's hymn praising God. They do not appear on this page by accident. Because these names are in dry-point, it suggests that they were not patrons of the Church or their names would have been written in ink. The names could only have been etched by someone with access to the St. Chad Gospels, intimating a monk or nun. If these names were etched by nuns, it provides evidence that women worked in the scriptorium at Lichfield.

17 Charles-Edwards and McKee, "Lost Voices," 81–82.

Figure 2.2. Spectral enhanced images showing recovery of dry-point writing, PTM file. Left: *Wulfun*, *Alchelm*, and *Eadric*, three names of Anglo-Saxon men, page 217, St. Chad Gospels. Right: *Wulfild*, one of three names of Anglo-Saxon women, page 226, St. Chad Gospels.

angle of lighting. For example, if raking light is below and mirrors the slant of the cross-stroke of the *N*, the *N* turns into an *H*. If the directional lighting moves to approximately a forty-degree angle to the cross-stroke, the *N* appears, allowing the letter to be properly identified (Web Fig. 2.11). *UN* completes the Anglo-Saxon name *Wulfun*.

Further into this page, RTI reveals additional dry-point. It is nestled above and below the feet of a beast. Above, the dry-point is the Anglo-Saxon name Wulfmaer (Web Fig. 2.12). Below, the dry-point is puzzling. It appears as if three Es, the second one perhaps two Es, one offset and overlaid on another. The last letter seems to be a B. The nature of these lines encourages me to question if these etchings represent a scribe or scribes testing their stylus and the hardness of the parchment, echoing the practice of scribes testing a newly cut nib in the margins before continuing.[18]

Such reasoning could explain the difficulty in identifying these letters and others discovered by Charles-Edwards in the lower margin on page 221.[19] He noticed what he best identified as *Past* and *+icc*. The *+icc* echoes the three *E*'s appearing above. However, RTI reveals further dry-point below the first group of letters and in the middle of the lower border (Web Fig. 2.13). The letters on the left appear as if a cross and an *L*. The letters in the middle appears as if *efry*. Occurring between these groups are a series of short, downward cuts and some less deeply etched marking. Some of this dry-point could represent testing the stylus and parchment. However, the middle letters, such as the *efry*, partially echo words that the scribe has written below. In a conversation and ensuing email exchange with Michelle Brown, she provides another viable possibility:

> In accordance with established practice in the manufacture of medieval manu-scripts, this would usually suggest that the preliminary version, in hardpoint or metalpoint, served as a draft, a trial or a guide to instruct a scribe, rubricator or

---

18 Kwakkel, "Doodles."

19 Charles-Edward and McKee, "Lost Voices," 80, 84.

artist in what to write or paint. In this case, however, given the inexpert nature of the hardpoint version and the scribal expertise of the hand repeating it in ink, and given the legal context of the textual content, it is perhaps more likely that the hardpoint represents the act of witnessing or performing a legal transaction, written by the grantor as a performative act before witnesses. When drawing up Anglo-Saxon charters the parties concerned and their witnesses would sometimes, it seems, write their own signs, even if a scribe wrote out their names, and at least one surviving example retains a draft witness list appended to the final version "in fine."[20]

Brown's reasoning is convincing. And as she points out, multiple things might be going on. Although dry-point generates its share of questions, having RTI provides a major advantage: other scholars can view it and participate in unraveling its mysteries.[21]

While RTI provides other valuable visual information for scholarship, such as rulings and hair follicles (Web Fig. 2.14), none of its information is more important than that which contributes to caring for these precious medieval survivors. In a regular digital image, surface details become flattened, revealing minimal evidence about the condition of inks and pigments. Conversely, RTI grants insight into their condition. For the St. Chad Gospels, pigment loss is a concern. Intensified by layering and encouraged by water-damage, loss of pigments requires monitoring and strategic intervention. An RTI generated normals visualization provides a quick assessment of rising pigments. Areas that reflect light at an angle near parallel to the page appear as a dark shade of red, green, or blue (Web Fig. 2.15). Such false-colour representation provides a warning for pigments that have risen dramatically from the page and are at risk. They can be further studied in the default and specular enhanced view for better assessing needed action (Web Fig. 2.15). Moreover, capturing and documenting surface details establishes a benchmark for recognizing future changes and evaluating them, alerting the need for intercessions.

The experience of any artistic expression is dependent upon materiality. RTI brings this materiality to the forefront. Within the Insular tradition, artists continually innovated, building on past artistic practices to heighten their visual glorification of God and portray meaning. In the St. Chad Gospels one way that the artists achieved this was by layering pigment. Throughout the manuscript, layered pigments generate a complexity of colour for enriched visual expression and meaning. For example, the scepter held by Luke (page 218) is coloured with an underlayer of a brownish pigment (likely either orchil or orcein) and overpainted with the green pigment verdigris. The colours suggests foliage, as do the fourteen interlaced strands that construct the top of the scepter, ending in elongated trefoil. Viewed in person or an RTI rendering, the texture of the lush green verdigris, accented

---

20 Brown, "Dry-Point." Also see Brown, "The Book as Sacred Space"; Brown, "Images"; Brown, *The Book*; Brown, *The Lindisfarne*.

21 For the RTI gallery, visit https://lichfield.ou.edu/st-chad-gospels/rti. Gianpaulo Palma, Visual Computing Lab of ISTI-CNR, developed this web RTI viewer (GNU General Public License): http://vcg.isti.cnr.it/rti/webviewer.php. However, I worked with Noah Adler to add specular enhancement: https://github.com/UK-AS-HIVE/media_rti.

Figure 2.3. Luke's scepter, page 218, St. Chad Gospels. Left: Lighting directly above the page. Right: Lighting from upper-right-hand side.

by the brownish pigment where verdigris has cracked and broken free, readily suggests a tree, whether the scepter as a tree of life or a reference to a verse in Luke. Such verses include "For every tree is known by its fruit" (6:44) and "a grain of mustard seed, which a man took and cast into his garden: and it grew and became a great tree, and the birds of the air lodged in the branches" (13:19) (Fig. 2.3 or Web Fig. 2.16). Visual references to scripture are a hallmark of Insular imagery.[22] The muted representation of artistic expression in regular digital images makes such references less noticeable and compelling.

Furthermore, RTI captures perhaps the most stunning artistic expression in Insular illuminated manuscripts: the play of light. The use of the yellow pigment orpiment mirrors the use of gold in Byzantine manuscripts, physically emulating the light of divine wisdom.[23] Capturing orpiment's texture and shimmer in shifting light is significant for capturing its artistic expression. Artists would have anticipated this shifting, a manuscript regularly lit by flicking candlelight. While RTI does not reproduce the effect of candlelight, it provides the opportunity to shift light, providing a more natural viewing experience. Shifts in light

---

22 Connolly, *Beed: On the Temple*; Pulliam, *Word and Image*; Endres, "Oh Lord make haste."

23 While I have had good success capturing a gold decorated initial in a book of hours, RTI generally has difficulty capturing shiny metals. Lindsay MacDonald has made breakthroughs in this area (MacDonald et al., "Modelling the Appearance"). Also, a team at the DHLab, University of Basel, has developed a new RTI method for capturing glossy surfaces (Fornaro et al., "Enhanced Reflectance").

can make material features more vibrant and change a sense of artistic expression, such as the dots of pigment constructing three crosses within Luke's halo (Web Fig. 2.17). In regular digital images, uniform lighting conceals surface details and adds a foreign static lighting to the experience. Such an unnatural element, while providing a valuable condition for examining and recovering some aspects of a manuscript, hides others. In this case, it hides the artistic and meaningful play of a manuscript and light.

In Chapter 1, I discuss recovery of erased content on page 141, the last page of Matthew's gospel. While RTI did not expose indentations that reveal further erased content, it did provide views to assess findings from the chapter. To begin, I examined the erased area applying specular enhancement, with colour shading set at 0 to increase contrast. This view confirmed serious scraping along the middle length of the area, suggesting erasure. It also confirmed the shape of the bird near the border, on the right-hand side (Web Fig. 2.18). Additionally, RTI makes evident that indentations from the opposite side (portrait of Mark) do not generate lines for the bird. Reversing and overlaying the decoration from Mark's portrait demonstrates the independence of major lines (Web Fig. 2.19). Magnifying the bird and examining it through various views further supports this independence: angled lighting and no enhancement, various spectral views, and overlaying the opposite page (Web Fig. 2.20). One direction of lighting does make the bird largely disappear; however, such an angle can generally be found. RTI generates evidence that the bird is caused by markings from its own side of the page.

Discerning erased text remains difficult. However, a spectral view, with and without colour shading, provides a strong indication of text running below and beginning at the *c* of *saeculi* and to the end of the first *finit*. While this text is still not legible, it appears more noticeably than it does through multispectral imaging and alternative colour spaces (Web Fig. 2.21). When I adjust the directional lighting and specular enhancement, I see some areas of the erased text more distinctly but lose others. The normals visualization provides less information (Web Fig. 2.22).

In RTI renderings, the pointing finger is likewise viewable, located below and between the *i* and *t* of the first *finit*. Its survival is likely due to its proximity to the *i* and *t* (Web Fig. 2.23). However, RTI also demonstrates how the impression of a finger could be caused by the chance scrapings of an erasure. With recoveries, caution is always in order. Also, examining the whole page is important. This can reveal anomalies in the parchment and its preparation. For example, the bottom margin reveals such scrapings but without the same level of discolouration and sense of an erasure (Web Fig. 2.24). In the erased area, some of the marks from scraping are likely due to the preparation of the parchment. This complicates recovery. Page 141 provides a good example of the difficult task of retrieving lost content, demonstrating the value of having alternative digital techniques for cross-referencing and chipping away at a mystery.

Concluding Comments

To miss the rich materiality of a manuscript is to miss its wonder. Whether the dark flow of iron gall ink against the creamy richness of vellum or the dynamic combination of triskeles and interlaced beasts forming an incipit, the totality of a page is breathtaking. However, this totality is dependent upon surface details. When a manuscript is intimately examined, these details resonate, making their intricacies seem "the result of work, not of men, but of angels."[24] Within the surface details lie aesthetic splendor and secrets. As I demonstrated in Chapter 1, exceptional benefits derive from uniform lighting and MSI. Through them, damaged content can be regained. However, scholars must recognize what is lost. Unified lighting negates the effect of a significant aspect of an illuminated manuscript: its play of light. Such play is essential to artistic expression, but it also makes surface details known. RTI restores this play, and in so doing captures surface details, providing visual information about rulings, hair follicles, rising pigments, and notoriously difficult to see dry-point writing. By providing a heightened digital encounter with materiality, RTI makes available irreplaceable information for understanding a manuscript and its medieval past.

New developments in RTI are further increasing its potential. A trend in the development of advanced imaging technologies is to increase their capabilities for what they already do well. Researchers working with RTI are bucking this trend. They have taken up innovative work that integrates other advanced imaging techniques, such as MSI with RTI.[25] Two projects that have generated good results are the Jubilees Palimpsest Project, Todd Hanneken,[26] and Reflectance Imaging for Cultural Heritage Project (RICH), KU Leuven.[27] Because capturing multiple frequencies of light for forty-five or more lighting positions is too time consuming for highlight RTI, both projects have had to solve difficulties related to domes: portability and accommodating large manuscripts. Working with Ken Boydston of MegaVision Inc., Hanneken has experimented with a virtual dome, constructed of an arc (eight feet in diameter) that moves banks of lights (capable of eight to sixteen lighting patterns) into necessary positions.[28] This solution provides portability and flexibility for larger manuscripts. The RICH Project, working with multiple collaborators, has developed a Multispectral Portable Light Dome. It contains 228 different LED lights, capturing frequencies of 365nm, 465nm, 523nm, 623nm, and 850nm. To have flexibility with manuscripts, the dome is secured slightly above them.[29] Its software can also extract 3D data.[30] Both of these projects demonstrate the dynamic nature of RTI and the potential for integrating it with other advanced imaging technologies.

---

24 Cambrensis, *The History and Topography*, 84.

25 RTI has a history of taking advantage of nonvisible light. Altering a camera to capture infrared frequencies has been a common practice for art historians and archaeologists. The ability of infrared to capture damaged carbon-based materials or penetrate below layers can provide significant visual information, this information made more vivid through RTI's mathematical enhancements. For example, see the discussion of Antonio Cosentino about its benefits for examining mural paintings and historical graffiti (Cosentino et al., "Innovative Imaging").

26 Hanneken, "New Technology."

27 Watteeuw et al., "Light, Shadows and Surface."

28 Hanneken, "Spectral RTI."

29 For a video demonstration of the Portable Light Dome, visit https://vimeo.com/175578404.

30 Watteeuw et al., "Light, Shadows and Surface," 1–2. However, captured 3D data is limited because the object and camera maintain a static position. Therefore, if a page has dramatic contours, full details are not captured where the page is more vertical to the camera.

Although these innovations are exciting, there is no reason for scholars to wait for them. Currently, highlight RTI is extremely effective and affordable. It is never too soon to document the condition of surface details and assess preservation needs. Likewise, it is never too soon to acquire more information for scholarship. Surface details contain essential information that is lost to regular digitization. RTI provides it. As this chapter demonstrates, a prime example is dry-point writing. In the case of the St. Chad Gospels, dry-point provides names that are significant for the history of the manuscript but also for understanding the larger history of medieval times. The names of three Anglo-Saxon women on page 226 suggests that women worked in the scriptorium at Lichfield, accounting for them having access to the manuscript and the skill to etch their names. These names raise questions as to whether other manuscripts contain the names of women. If so, do they tend to accompany particular verses? How does this evidence relate to other evidence of female scribes?[31] Until scholars have access to this data, the value of its witnessing is obscured, echoing what Michelle Brown writes of the name *Dark Ages*, "in which the only darkness is the cloud of our own unknowing."[32] RTI can shine some light through this cloud. It can aid with discoveries concealed in surface details. It can help celebrate a manuscript as a play of light, significant for encountering and embracing these artistic marvels from the Age of Visual Wonder.

Note

* All Web Figures referred to in this chapter can be accessed at: billendres.com/book/chap2/chap2.html.

---

31 Evidence of women working as scribes continues to increase (Backhouse, "The Female Scribe"; Brown, "Female Book-Ownership"; Beach, *Women as Scribes*).

32 Brown, "An Early Outbreak," 6.

Chapter 3

THE OTHERWISE UNKNOWABLE: DIGITIZING AND COMPARING HISTORICAL PHOTOGRAPHS*

FOR MONITORING CHANGES in manuscripts, scholars and conservators have long recognized the value of photography.[1] In the 1980s, to check for damage, conservators at the British Library compared earlier photographs of the Lindisfarne Gospels to the manuscript.[2] However, assessing cultural heritage through photographs has its origins in the earliest days of photography. For example, shortly after Louis-Jacques-Mandé Daguerre successfully demonstrated his daguerreotype in Paris (1839), the French Commission des Monuments Historiques hired five photographers to capture images of the nation's architectural heritage. Responsible for its preservation, the Commission wished to assess the conditions of historic sites throughout France, many not accessible by rail. This lack of access by rail echoes access to the past conditions of manuscripts. Both require photography. Now, the digital opens ways for understanding these past conditions and the aging processes of manuscripts by extending what can be known from historical photographs.

Digitized photographs provide three major advantages over printed ones. First, once digitized, photographs can be overlaid, and the transparency of the top image adjusted. This eliminates reliance on side-by-side comparisons and looking back-and-forth, making losses easier to identify. Second, while overlay benefits identifying losses, it becomes more beneficial when images align. Because the content of digitized images is malleable, such alignment is possible, a digital process called registration. Through overlay and transparency, comparing registered images makes smaller differences more apparent. It also enables identifying differences through computer-assisted means, such as subtracting one image from another. Through subtraction, resulting images reveal miniscule changes that otherwise likely go unnoticed, such as losses measuring .1 mm in diameter. Third, digitizing historical photographs preserves them in a digital form, allowing them to be collected and redundantly stored, safeguarding their irreplaceable content.

In this chapter, I demonstrate the value of and provide an approach for digitizing, registering, and comparing historical photographs. I make this case, however, not simply to propose a practice worthy of becoming best practice whenever digitizing a manuscript. Because of its unprecedented benefits, I want to encourage its practice even when a major digitization of a manuscript is not at hand. Information gained from digitizing historical photographs is far too important to ignore and too valuable to risk losing. In my work with the St. Chad Gospels, I demonstrate contributions from a range of past

---

1 Stolow, *Conservation and Exhibitions*; Schuler, "The Use of Photography," 3.

2 Helen Shenton, conversation at The Wandering Word: The Travels of Insular Manuscripts, Trinity College, Dublin, Ireland, May 5–7, 2016.

photographic methods, from nineteenth-century printed images to a copy from a 1920s photostat machine (the precursor to the photocopier). Considered less advanced, earlier technologies are regularly assumed to preserve inferior information. However, their precision is consistently surprising, and the content they document is irreplaceable. By examining these historical photographs of the St. Chad Gospels, I reveal trends in aging, effects of conservation treatments, and vulnerabilities for the manuscript. I enhance this information with the likes of 3D renderings, contributing evidence about contours and how they affect losses. This added information demonstrates the value of employing a range of advanced imaging techniques, a major argument of this book. Finally, I argue that digitizing and comparing historical photographs is not solely beneficial to an individual manuscript. When gathered, this information allows comparisons among manuscripts, expanding knowledge and increasing understanding across manuscripts, leading to better care for all.

Decisions and Method

For preserving and studying cultural heritage, registering images is enjoying increased attention. However, this attention is directed toward another purpose: generating 3D models. Popular approaches such as photogrammetry[3] require registration because they rely on aligned and overlapping segments of a series of photographs. In an early and well-known example, a team from ETH Zürich generated 3D reconstructions of two sixth-century Buddhas. These Buddhas, one the tallest in the world, were destroyed by the Taliban in 2001. To generate their models, the team aligned a variety of overlapping images, including tourists' photographs from 1965 to 1969, metric images from 1970,[4] and photographs collected from the internet.[5] These photographs represented various angles and distances and types of cameras, requiring complicated alignments before the team could produce 3D models. Today, advances in photogrammetric software, which includes algorithms for registration, support generating 3D models with a smartphone.[6]

In digitizing manuscripts, registration has played limited but key roles. For example, early MSI required adjusting photographs for geometric distortion. This distortion originated from filters needed to block frequencies of light except the one targeted for an image. If left uncorrected, when red, green, and blue images were merged into a colour

---

3 Photogrammetry is a scientific method that uses a series of overlapping photographs to make measurements. Its outputs include maps and 3D models.

4 Metric images are produced with specialized cameras. The coordinates within the photograph can be used to calculate accurate measurements.

5 Grün et al., "Photogrammetric Reconstruction," 183.

6 Available free apps for smartphones continues to change, as companies shift from supplying successful apps for free to charging for them. At this writing, Qlone, TRnio, and Scann3D represent good free options. Pay options such as Agrisoft PhotoScan and Autodesk ReMake generate 3D models from images taken with a smartphone or digital camera. They run on a laptop or desktop computer and require images to be downloaded for processing.

photograph, the distortion caused blurriness. For multispectral imaging, the introduction of LED lighting changed this. LED lighting permits control over the frequency of light emitted, eliminating the need for filters. Registration is still required, however, for some advanced imaging techniques, such as ultraviolet reflectography[7] and when capturing fluorescence.[8]

Conversely, developing and refining techniques for registering images represents a necessity and long-standing area of research in medicine.[9] This makes medical imaging a good place to turn for solutions. Medical professionals have a crucial need to compare content in images taken over time, such as monitoring tumors and lesions. But perhaps more importantly, registration is necessary for aligning complementary content from varying imaging technologies. These technologies capture different aspects of the materiality of the human body. For example, a doctor needs magnetic resonance imaging for the outline of lesions but a CT scan to calculate dose distributions.[10] Because registering medical images represents similar problems to those for registering historical photographs of manuscripts, solutions from medical imaging provide viable approaches.

To register historical photographs, software needs to address two types of alignments or *transformations*: global and local. To align images, global transformations use linear mathematical approaches. They are proportional and affect the whole image. Such transformations adjust for perspective, scale, and rotation. When photographs are taken on different dates and with different equipment, the camera is never positioned at an identical angle to or distance from a manuscript; therefore, perspective, rotation, and scale need adjusted. The second type of methods, local, also known as elastic, do not affect the whole image. More complex, these methods stretch and shrink content in localized areas, transforming or *unwarping* it to bring targeted content into alignment.[11]

Materiality dictates the types of transformations needed. Because manuscripts are made from parchment, both global and local methods are necessary. As mentioned, global methods are always needed to adjust for differences in the location of the camera in relations to a manuscript, affecting perspective, scale, and rotation. But for parchment, local methods are also required. As an organic substance, parchment fluctuates. In the case of the St. Chad Gospels, its pages fluctuated dramatically. Early water damage and prolonged dampness caused the pages to warp, a condition known as cockling.[12] Severe ridges and valleys dominated the once level vellum. In 1962, Roger Powell flattened the

---

7 For ultraviolet reflectography, the source lighting strikes the surface at an angle; the camera is positioned at a mirrored angle to capture the results (Obrutsky et al., "Reflectography," 2004).

8 Hollaus et al., "Multispectral Image Acquisition," 33.

9 van den Elsen et al., "Medical Imaging Matching," 26–39.

10 van den Elsen et al., "Medical Imaging Matching," 26.

11 Goshtasby, *Image Registration*, 301–10.

12 Roger Powell surmised that the edges of pages were trimmed during the 1707 binding to save the St. Chad Gospels from mould, a symptom of its prolonged dampness (Powell, "The Lichfield," 159).

pages, dramatically shifting the coordinates of content back toward their original state (Web Fig. 3.1).

But dramatic changes aside, parchment constantly fluctuates. It is highly sensitive to changes in relative humidity, a condition known as hygroscopicity. Increases cause it to readily absorb moisture from the air, expanding as it does.[13] This would not be such a problem if the expansion were proportional. However, vellum lacks uniformity, varying in thickness and concentration of fibers. When vellum expands, it expands unevenly across the surface of a page, causing photographs taken when relative humidity differs to preserve content with differing coordinates. For manuscripts, this is significant because earlier historical photographs were generally taken outside of climate-controlled environments.[14]

To register images, one of the crucial decisions is choosing the set of photographs to function as references. A reference is the image to which others are mathematically aligned. Selecting references is not always obvious and varies, depending upon available historical photographs, scholarly questions, materiality of the manuscript, and state of the manuscript when photographs were taken. For example, if a manuscript has seriously deteriorated or incurred damage since early photographs were taken, early photographs might serve best as references, providing a framework for mapping later losses and understanding them.

For the St. Chad Gospels, I have nine sets of images from which to choose, three of which are complete sets (1929, 1962, and 2010):

- 1887—photographs, selected pages, F. H. A. Scrivener's *Codex S. Ceaddea Latinus*
- 1911—photographs, selected pages, unknown circumstances
- 1929—photostat copy, Llyfrgell Genedlaethol Cymru / The National Library of Wales, Aberystwyth
- 1956[15]—colour slides, selected pages, likely Br. Frowin Oslender, Maria Laach Abbey, Germany
- 1962—photographs, Conway Library, Courtauld Institute of Art, London, England[16]
- 1962—colour photographs, selected pages, P. Belzeaux (Zodiaque), for Françoise Henry[17]

---

13 Clarkson, "Rediscovering Parchment," 5–6; Woods, "Conservation Treatments," 222–24.

14 For the St. Chad Gospels, the 2003 and 2010 images make for a good comparison. Both benefitted from Roger Powell's flattening. The 2003 images were taken in a climate-controlled environment at the British Library. The 2010 images were taken at the end of June in the server's vestry at Lichfield Cathedral, the humidity controlled as best possible with an industrial-grade dehumidifier. When the 2003 images are adjusted for scale, perspective, and rotation, relative humidity accounts for the differences.

15 It indicates earliest date supported by archival information in Lichfield Cathedral Library.

16 All of the black-and-white film negatives are available at the Courtauld Institute. Roger Powell also reports that the Courtauld Institute took some photographs in colour. However, the Courtauld has no surviving evidence of these photographs (Powell, "The Lichfield," 159).

17 To the best of my knowledge, only six pages were photographed: 5, 142, 143, 218, 219, and 220. Comparing them to the 1962 photographs, I discovered no differences in loss of pigment between them.

- 1982—colour transparencies, selected pages, Sonia Halliday Photo Library
- 2003—digital images, British Library (in collaboration with Lichfield Cathedral, England, and Llandeilo Fawr, Wales)[18]
- 2010—digital images (multispectral and 3D), team led by Bill Endres.

In the end, I chose images from 2010. If my interest had been assessing the extent to which pages were retaining their flatness, I would have chosen the 1962 black-and-white photographs. These photographs capture the pages immediately after Powell flattened them and before he rebound the manuscript. The 1962 photographs represent the pages in their flattest and most restored state. Following Powell's work, the St. Chad Gospels was displayed in a humidity monitored but not controlled case; therefore, slight warping likely returned. Also, in capturing pages in their unbound state, the 1962 photographs are free from the swell caused by the binding when the manuscript is opened (Web Fig. 3.2). In later images, this swell alters the coordinates of content.

The materiality of pigment, however, makes the 1962 photographs less viable as references. Black-and-white images inadequately represent bright colours. In the St. Chad Gospels, part of the artistic palette is the bright yellow pigment orpiment. It is meant to emulate the glow of divine wisdom. A good amount of this pigment has been lost; therefore, it is highly important to monitor it. In the 1962 photographs, orpiment is nearly indistinguishable from accumulated dirt and blemishes in the vellum. This makes colour images crucial, providing a benchmark for assessing orpiment and other brightly coloured pigments. As a potential reference, the 1956 slides provide early colour images, but they are limited in number, only twelve pages. However, they also suffer from lost content in the gutter, likely caused by the pre-1962 binding, its tightness prohibiting the manuscript from being opened adequately for photography.

Furthermore, selecting the 2010 images provides a practical benefit. As discussed in Chapter 1, when I digitized the manuscript, I generally captured images for thirteen frequencies of light, from ultraviolet to infrared. If earlier photographs are selected as references, all of these multispectral images would need to be registered, too. For the whole manuscript, this amounts to roughly two thousand images. Therefore, the 2010 images provide the logical choice, generating a benchmark for brightly coloured pigments and eliminating the need to register the thirteen multispectral images per page.

Various scholarly questions motivate my comparing historical photographs; however, as I discuss in Chapter 4 and an earlier article, a large motive is reciprocity, insuring that Lichfield Cathedral benefit from my digitization.[19] Digitizing a manuscript stresses it. It presents multiple risks, not the least of which is turning pages and increasing opportunities for fragile chips of pigment to break free. Generating any information to understand aging better and identify pages in need of special care aids in offsetting

---

18 Although the complete manuscript was imaged, sixty-four images are currently missing.
19 Endres, "Imaging Sacred Artefacts."

these risks, contributing to the longevity of the manuscript central to the community of Lichfield Cathedral.

To understand the aging of the St. Chad Gospels, trends need to be assessed before and after 1962, pre- and post-flattening. Since 1962, the manuscript has aged differently. Theoretically, flattening pages and replacing the binding alleviates stress. A tight binding restricts pages from turning freely, generating heightened tension across the surface of a page when turned. Pigments are rigid and adhere to vellum, not etching into and bonding with it like inks. When pages cockle, they place stress on pigments. If the adhesion holds, pigments crack and find a new balance on the vellum. Cracked pigments, however, are in a weakened state; chips are more likely to break free. By flattening the pages of the St. Chad Gospels, Powell eliminated this stress.

But Powell also strengthened the bond of fragile pigments. Following best practices of his day, he treated pigments rising from the vellum with liquid nylon, increasing their consolidation.[20] Liquid nylon is no longer the standard for conservators; however, understanding its effectiveness helps to assess future risks for the St. Chad Gospels and other manuscripts treated with it. For the St. Chad Gospels, therefore, two patterns need compared to assess its aging: one before 1962 and one after. Such a comparison is vital because it exposes current trends and provides crucial information about the effects of flattening and rebinding on aging.

To compare trends before and after 1962, commensurate periods are needed. To provide the longest periods within the constraints of the irregular photographic efforts (1887, 1911, 1929, 1956, 1962, 1982, 2003, and 2010), the two best choices are from 1911 to 1956 and 1962 to 2010. This generates periods of forty-five and forty-eight years. I eliminated 1887 as a possible beginning point because only three photographs exist from this effort: one major decorated page and two textual pages. Still, the 1887 photographs provide crucial supportive information. Also, I treat the six-year period from 1956 to 1962 as a separate period. As its own period, it provides crucial information about losses occurring during the flattening and rebinding, activities that might cause an uncharacteristically high rate of loss.

While neither the 1911 or 1956 efforts capture the whole manuscript, they include the major decorated pages and a few textual pages. In addition, the 1911 photographs have a sharpness that rivals the 1962 photographs and 2010 digital images. 1911 to 1956 represents a forty-five-year period and is commensurate to the span of forty-eight years from 1962 to 2010. Having periods of nearly fifty years allows a relatively large span to offset years with abnormally high or low losses. Such norming through larger periods is important because limited information is known to adjust for other circumstances or events that impacted aging.

To understand aging further, periods can be divided into smaller slices, contingent on remaining photographic efforts. For example, the 1982 transparencies represent a near mid-point from 1962 to 2010, dividing that period into slices of twenty and twenty-eight

---

20 For consolidation, current materials include gelatine (Speta, "The Conservation of the Hussite Codex," 22–23) and sturgeon glue (Pataki-Hundt, "Conservation Treatment,"154–55).

years. These slices can be made commensurate by dividing the number of losses by the number of years, generating a proportional comparison. Comparing these commensurate results can help to assess whether aging is accelerating.

Before registering all of the images, I carried out preliminary comparisons to test the validity of my approach. For all major decorated pages from 1911, 1956,[21] and 1962, I adjusted them globally, using the 2010 images as references. To assess losses to minor decorated initials, I included five water-damaged textual pages from throughout the manuscript. During preliminary comparisons of historical images, I found that losses could be easily identified by adjusting the transparency of the top overlaid image. Also, I found that identifying smaller losses was easier if I enhanced globally adjusted images by aligning the width of pages. Finally, I found that global adjustments benefited understanding where cockling warped the content in pre-1962 images.[22]

Preliminary results confirmed that pigments represent the most vulnerable feature. However, raising concerns was that some major decorated pages showed continuing losses. These pages include the portraits of Mark and Luke (pages 142 and 218) and their incipits (pages 143 and 221). Two major pages showed miniscule losses: the Chi-Rho (page 5) and Cross-Carpet (page 220). For textual pages, pages 141 and 217 showed rare losses for minor decorated initials. These pages have significant features and generate much interest. Also, they form the opposite side of portrait pages. Therefore, they incur added viewing and stress. Finally, to further understand the uncovered trends, I globally registered Luke's portrait and incipit for the other photographic efforts. Comparisons of these pages showed that more recent pigment loss remains below pre-1956 levels, but it appears to be increasing. These results proved the soundness of my method and the value of pursuing my more thorough study.

An Open-Source Solution

In this book, one of my goals is to present open-source solutions for digitally presenting, preserving, and studying manuscripts. In Chapter 1, I demonstrate the value of ImageJ for the post-processing of images to recover damaged content. In the current chapter, I return to it as a robust solution for registering images. Developed by the US National Institute of Health, ImageJ is designed for scientifically analyzing images rather than editing them. To assess aging, however, I added a manual step, globally adjusting images, to gain a better sense of cockling. For this, I turned to Photoshop, image editing software. For an open-source alternative, GIMP provides a good solution.

---

21 To supply Lichfield Cathedral with much anticipated results, I registered selected images in 2010. I released a portion of this work online. In 2014, I returned to Lichfield to digitize the 1956 slides. By globally aligning and overlaying historical images, I was struck by how much information was revealed when I adjusted the top image's transparency. After digitizing the 1956 slides, I completed the core stage of this study. I have enhanced its results as I acquire further images, such as the 1982 transparencies of Sonia Halliday.

22 See https://lichfield.ou.edu/st-chad-gospels/historical-image-overlays.

With manual adjustments, my approach to registering historical images takes five-steps. First, I placed all images for a single page into a separate folder. Because the 2010 RGB images are references, I do not need to include the thirteen multispectral images; they are already aligned. Second, using an automated script in Photoshop, I load a folder's images as layers into a Photoshop file. This creates a single file of images for a page, stacked in layers. Third, I adjust each image using the rotate, scale, and perspective tools (under *Edit > Transform*). I adapt the transparency as needed to make the adjustments. Photoshop has global alignment algorithms, but I ignore them to gain a better sense of the cockling. Once each stacked layer is globally aligned, I save it as an image. Overlaying globally aligned images provides a sense of how cockling distorts content (Web Fig. 3.1 and Web Fig. 3.3).

My fourth and fifth steps include semi-automated registration. Registration can be fully automated, but better results generally occur with semi-automated approaches. These approaches are computerized, but they have built-in breaks for human interven-tion. Such a break occurs between automated feature extraction and digitally unwarping the content of a target image. For the fourth step, I use a plugin called Feature Extraction (developed by Stephan Saalfeld). It automatically identifies corresponding points between two images. Feature extraction relies on two main approaches, SIFT (Scale Invariant Feature Transform) and MOPS (Multiscale Oriented Patches). For pages of manuscripts, SIFT most effectively identifies corresponding features. After running the plugin, small circles with a crossing vertical and horizontal line appear on the images. These circles mark corresponding points (Web Fig. 3.4 and Web Fig. 3.5). For registra-tion, these points are called *landmarks*. Landmarks can be manually placed, but such work is time-consuming. Saalfeld's Feature Extraction plugin saves substantial time, automatically identifying and marking correspondences.[23] Landmarks increase the accuracy of alignment.

Saving further time, Saalfeld's Feature Extraction plugin automatically makes its landmarks available to BUnwarpJ, the registration plugin I use in ImageJ. When BUnwarpJ launches, my fifth and final step, the corresponding points are retained. Upon examining the landmarks, if I find them satisfactory, I run BUnwarpJ. If not, BUnwarpJ allows me to set further landmarks. Because of cockling and the pre-1962 binding, images captured prior to 1962 tend to have content nearest the gutter regularly com-pressed or cut off. This makes automated feature extraction difficult in these areas. In such cases, I manually create a few landmarks on the reference image. As I create them, BUnwarpJ automatically generates them for the target image; however, because its con-tent is warped, these landmarks on the target image must be moved to align them with the exact corresponding points (Web Fig. 3.7, Web Fig. 3.8, and Web Fig. 3.9).

---

23 While Saalfeld's Feature Extraction plugin performs impressively, assessing accuracy for com-puterized processes is important. Using overlay, I compared landmarks and found few errors. Web Fig. 3.6 shows one slightly larger error. Areas with narrow, swirling lines, such as these triskeles decorating the Chi-Rho, seem to cause more problems when the plugin tries to identify corresponding points.

Again, once I am satisfied with landmarks, I begin BUnwarpJ. Generally, it takes the plugin six to fifteen minutes to align the target image. Textual pages take longer, having more details (strokes of letters) to align. BUnwarpJ generates a registered image and additional visual information, including a helpful line grid showing directional changes required to unwarp the target image (Web Fig. 3.10).

Because digital images represent visual information in numbers, basic mathematical operations can be used to compare images and aid in identifying losses. Graphics software, such as ImageJ, have tools for performing these operations, such as subtracting the values of corresponding pixels between two images to generate a new one. In ImageJ, this functionality is provided by the *Image Calculator* under the *Process* menu item. To make results more vivid, I convert registered images to greyscale, adjusting tonal levels with an adjustment curve.[24] Curves function nonlinearly and allow me to target specific lighting conditions, leading to more precise tonal matching across a set of images. After subtracting images, similar tone increases the contrast of differences, making smaller losses much more evident.

Choosing which image is subtracted from the other matters. In greyscale, each pixel has a value from 0 to 255, from black to white. Vellum is whitish. Its light cream colour has a relatively high value. Generally, pigments are darker and have lower values. To generate contrast for lost pigment, subtracting an earlier image from a later one is significant. Areas that show pigment in both images result in subtracted values near zero. The same occurs for vellum. A resulting image, therefore, will be largely black. However, where pigment has broken free, subtracting lower values for pigment in earlier photographs from higher values where pigment has broken free and vellum shows through generates relatively high values. These higher values appear whitish, resulting in losses standing out (Web Fig. 3.11, Web Fig. 3.12, and Web Fig. 3.13).

RGB images can be used; however, they generally do not produce contrast as acutely. For these images, each pixel has a value for red, green, and blue, and those three values are subtracted for each pixel (Web Fig. 3.14). Because I am trying to identify as small of areas of loss as possible, generating the best contrast is vital. Subtracting greyscale images has helped me to identify losses measuring 0.1 mm in diameter.

Results and Discussion

My initial examination of globally registered images demonstrated reduced losses since the 1961–1962 flattening of pages and rebinding; however, this is only the beginning of the story. Although losses have significantly decreased, visual information generated by subtracting fully registered images reveals a substantial number of miniscule losses. These losses measure from 0.3 to 0.1 mm in width (0.01 to 0.004 inches). I will refer to them as micro-losses. They account for the larger portion of losses for the period when the flattening occurred.

---

24 For this work, I revert to graphics editing software such as Photoshop.

Ascertaining trends requires a mix of complementary numeric data. To start, identifying and counting lost chips provides one indication of magnitude and a means for making comparisons. While not definitive, such an approach presents valuable information and is comparable to calculating the average for a set of numbers. An average presents one way to summarize and understand data. Finding the median, for instance, is another.

Varying precision in photographs makes identifying and counting lost chips a difficult and time-consuming process. Comparing any two digitized historical photographs can reveal false losses. This can occur for many reasons, whether deterioration of a film-based slide, inexactness in printing a negative, lack of sharpness due to cockling, or quality of the camera or lens. Therefore, to affirm a loss requires consulting the previous and prior historical photographs to the ones being compared—and sometimes more. Imprecise edges occur in all sets of photographs and vary within sets, some pages and areas of pages being precise while others less so. This inexactness is generally highest in the photostat copy and 1956 slides. A case in point is an area of lost pigment below the crossbar of the *N* on the second line of Mark's incipit (Web Fig. 3.15). It is shaped like Aladdin's lamp and appears smaller in the 1956 and 1929 images. If the 1956 image is subtracted from the 1962 image, the results show a loss in this area. To discern accurate information, not simply the prior 1929 image needs consulted but also the 1911 photograph, two images prior. The 1911 photograph provides the telling information, confirming that no loss has occurred.

For complementary numeric information, I measured the largest lost chip for each period. I would have preferred to calculate the total surface area of losses. However, performing such a calculation is far from trivial. For the total surface area of losses, computing the percentage of off-whites in subtracted images would not produce reliable results for three main reasons. First, anomalies and dirt would first need removed from images. The digitized 1956 slides, although carefully cleaned, are particularly rich in dust and dirt particles, as older slides generally are. Second, as discussed and demonstrated earlier, images representing imprecise edges in photographs produce false losses. Finally, differences in lighting produce differently lit surfaces and sometimes shimmer and glints in photographs. Because of the small-sized room where the 2010 digitization took place, lighting needed to be offset. This caused higher instances of glints than in other photographs.

Furthermore, when identifying micro-losses, the angle of light can cause the illusion of extra pigment. Layered pigments, as in the St. Chad Gospels, produce rises that cast varying shadows in different lighting. In black-and-white photographs, these shadows blend with the pigment and are difficult to differentiate. In colour images, these shadows can take on the hue of the pigment. Consulting RTI renderings provides guidance for sorting out these shadows. They emulate the effect of angles of light when viewing areas where pigments in photographs give the impression of having shifted (Web Fig. 3.16).

To calculate the total surface area of losses, a computerized method would first need to adjust images for dirt, shimmer, photographic imperfections, and imprecisions. This would require much human intervention. In addition, to make meaningful comparisons, the amount of pigment on a page would need to be calculated. This would allow for

Table 3.1. Number of lost chips of pigment from 1911 to 1956, 1956 to 1962, and 1962 to 2010 for Mark's incipit, Luke's incipit, Mark's portrait, Luke's portrait, and the Cross-Carpet page.

Number of Lost Chips	1911–1956	1956–1962	1962–2010**
Mark's Incipit	75	14	20
Luke's Incipit	72	13	20
Mark's Portrait*	75	14	20
Luke's Portrait	32	10	19
Cross-Carpet Page	28	2	11

* The number of lost chips for Mark's Portrait does not include losses occurring in the frame. These losses are the yellow pigment orpiment, which is impossible to discern in black-and-white photographs. Counting them in later images would have misrepresented losses.
** Details are generally more precise in 2003 and 2010 images, making micro-losses easier to identify.

calculating a percentage of loss. However, calculating the amount of pigment on a page would face similar difficulties to calculating the amount of lost pigment. Therefore, to make such calculations is impractical.

Lost pigment primarily occurs in five of the eight major decorated pages; therefore, I will start by providing numeric information for them: Mark's incipit, Luke's incipit, Mark's portrait, Luke's portrait, and the Cross-Carpet page.[25] Table 3.1 presents the number of chips lost by period. For visually comparing and gauging losses, Table 3.2 presents a bar chart of this information. However, this information might be understated. For instance, large lost chips might represent multiple chips breaking free at different times between photographic efforts. Therefore, these numbers provide a basis from which to begin to understand aging.

For lost chips, a dramatic decline occurs between the two main periods: 1911–1956 and 1962–2010. This decline suggests that Powell's flattening of pages and rebinding had a profound and positive impact on the aging of the manuscript. Cockling would have placed constant stress on pigments. But unfortunately, I cannot make a definitive assessment because no records exist to rule out other factors, such as handling of the manuscript during these times. Therefore, it is critical that similar studies for other manuscripts that have undergone flattening be done. Such studies would provide evidence for comparison and possible corroboration of results. Still, the decreased losses for these five decorated and vulnerable pages is dramatic, a decrease from 282 chips from 1911–1956 to 90 chips from 1962–2010. It represents an impressive 68 percent reduction.

---

25 After the manuscript was stolen, Matthew's incipit likely served as the cover for a number of years (Brown, "Lichfield/Llandeilo Gospels," 64). Therefore, little pigment remains. The Chi-Rho and evangelist symbols pages show few losses, having lost a fair amount of pigment prior to 1887 or, in the case of the Chi-Rho, the artist using coloured washes in areas rather than layered pigments.

Table 3.2. Bar graph of the number of lost chips of pigment from 1911 to 1956, 1956 to 1962, and 1962 to 2010 for Mark's incipit, Luke's incipit, Mark's portrait, Luke's portrait, and the Cross-Carpet page.

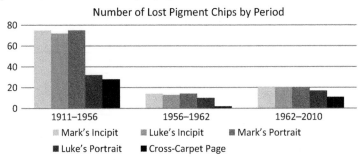

For the number of lost chips, the Cross-Carpet page shows a stark contrast to the two incipits and two portraits. While it lost pigment prior to 1911, the number of losses since is far less than the other major decorated pages. However, unlike the other pages, a technique of layered washes accounts for a fair amount of the decoration,[26] limiting the pigment that can be lost. Furthermore, most of the current losses occur in the frame, identified by Roosen-Runge and Werner as white lead glazed with folium.[27] However, this glaze is likely the lichen-based pigment orchil or orcein.

Powell's positive impact on aging is further demonstrated by a visual representation of the number and size of lost chips. Figure 3.1 or Web Fig. 3.17 and Web Fig. 3.18 provide visual information about losses for the incipit for Mark. Web Fig. 3.19 and Web Fig. 3.20 provide detailed views of line 1 of Mark's incipit. These representations are generated by converting images to greyscale for better contrast and subtracting the beginning image for a period from the ending one. The whitish areas inside circles represent lost chips. The circles and pointers distinguish losses from the whitish areas caused by dirt, lighting inconsistencies, anomalies in photographs, and differing precision of the various photographic technologies. The size of losses is noticeably smaller in the periods from 1956–1962 and 1962–2010.

Complementing the visual representations, additional perspective is gained by measuring the size of the largest lost chip for each period (Table 3.3). In four of the five pages, the largest loss occurs in the period from 1911 to 1956. The Cross-Carpet page is the anomaly, experiencing similar-sized losses for each period.

Because calculating the total surface area of losses is impractical, data about the size of the largest lost chip per page by period provides needed perspective. This data complements information about the number of chips, presenting an indicator of surface area to compare periods and understand the volume of shed pigment. For example, from 1911 to 1956, the number of lost chips for Luke's portrait makes it appear as if this page aged favourably: only thirty-two lost chips compared to seventy-five for Mark's portrait.

---

26 Brown, "The Lindisfarne," 277.

27 Roosen-Rung and Werner, "The Pictorial Technique."

Table 3.3. Largest lost chip of pigment from 1911 to 1956, 1956 to 1962, and 1962 to 2010 for Mark's incipit, Luke's incipit, Mark's portrait, Luke's portrait, and the Cross-Carpet page.

Largest Lost Chip	1911–1956	1956–1962	1962–2010
Mark's Incipit	2.1 × 2.4	0.4 × 0.9	0.4 × 0.5
Luke's Incipit	0.9 × 2.1	0.3 × 0.6*	0.8 × 1.3
Mark's Portrait	1.5 × 1.6	0.4 × 0.2	0.4 × 0.4
Luke's Portrait	3.1 × 6.6	0.4 × 0.7	0.4 × 0.7*
Cross-Carpet Page	0.5 × 1.8	0.9 × 1.7	0.9 × 1.6

All measurements represent longest width and height in millimetres, with width the first number.
*Triangular-shaped.

Figure 3.1. Incipit for Mark, page 143, St. Chad Gospels. Left: Identified losses by subtracting 1911 from 1956 image. Right: Identified losses by subtracting 1962 from 2010 image. Left: Ars liturgica e.K., Klosterverlag, D-56653 Maria Laach, 1956. Unknown, 1911. Right: Conway Library, The Courtauld Institute of Art, London, 1962. 2010 image reproduced by kind permission of the Chapter of Lichfield Cathedral.

However, the size of Luke's largest loss changes this assessment. It is roughly ten times the size of Mark's largest loss. Rectangular, it measures 6.6 mm in height and varies in width from 3.1 to 1.7 mm. Mark's lost chip measures 1.5 × 1.6 mm, but it is shaped like a church with a steeple (Web Fig. 3.21). Knowing this information changes the assessment of Luke's portrait, this page instead to have suffered some of the heaviest losses during the 1911–1956 period.

Table 3.4. Number of lost chips of pigment per year from 1911 to 1956, 1956 to 1962, and 1962 to 2010 for Mark's incipit, Luke's incipit, Mark's portrait, Luke's portrait, and the Cross-Carpet page.

Lost Chips Per Year	1911–1956	1956–1962	1962–2010
Mark's Incipit	1.67	2.33	0.42
Luke's Incipit	1.60	2.17	0.42
Mark's Portrait	1.67	2.33	0.42
Luke's Portrait	0.71	1.67	0.40
Cross-Carpet Page	0.62	0.33	0.23

In addition, the exceptionally large size of this chip makes it important to examine Luke's portrait further. The chip is the green pigment verdigris. Verdigris decorates a large portion of Luke's robe, covering five sections and his staff. In these sections, pigment is cracked into plates, some showing a tendency to rise. Past losses suggest that large pieces of this pigment broke free. Furthermore, verdigris is layered over a reddish wash and appears to have covered other sections of the robe, which now show slight residue of green. On other major decoration, verdigris is not found in this quantity, making it difficult to assess comparative vulnerability. But because this verdigris is at risk, it warrants close monitoring.

To provide better comparative assessment, Table 3.4 presents the number of chips lost per year. This enables a better sense of comparative losses for the period from 1956 to 1962.

As expected from the number of lost chips, 1962–2010 shows the lowest rates. The highest rates occur from 1956 to 1962, except for the Cross-Carpet page. Such rates raise questions about the effects of rebinding and flattening pages on pigments. Closely examining losses from 1956 to 1962 reveals that most of them are micro-losses. This suggests that smaller chips are more at risk during the hydrating and stretching of pages for their flattening. Because conservators would not have had information about micro-losses or been able to identify them, they would not have been unable to refine techniques to protect against their loss.

Powell's hydrating, stretching, and drying of pages appears far less traumatic to larger areas of pigment-at-risk than previous stresses to the manuscript, most notably from cockling. For largest lost chips, comparing 1956–1962 to the prior period, the sizes are notably smaller (Tab. 3.3). Furthermore, from 1962 to 2010, the largest lost chips are only marginally larger when compared to 1956–1962. This trend of smaller-sized lost chips for the 1962–2010 period probably results from two main causes. First, flattening the pages would have reduced the stress on pigments. Second, and likely a significant factor, Powell treated at-risk pigments with liquid nylon, increasing their consolidation.

To generate a more nuanced understanding of how pigments are aging since Powell's flattening, I compared the transparencies from 1982 to the 1962 and 2003 images and

Table 3.5. Number of lost chips of pigment from 1962 to 1982, 1982 to 2003, and 2003 to 2010 for Mark's incipit, Luke's incipit, Mark's portrait, Luke's portrait, and the Cross-Carpet page.

Number of Lost Chips	1962–1982	1982–2003	2003–2010**
Mark's Incipit	5	10	5
Luke's Incipit	6	9	5
Mark's Portrait*	20	0	0
Luke's Portrait	9	11	6
Cross-Carpet Page	9	1	1

Table 3.6. Number of lost chips of pigment per year from 1962 to 1982, 1982 to 2003, and 2003 to 2010 for Mark's incipit, Luke's incipit, Mark's portrait, Luke's portrait, and the Cross-Carpet page.

Lost Chips Per Year	1962–1982	1982–2003	2003–2010
Mark's Incipit	0.25	0.48	0.71
Luke's Incipit	0.30	0.43	0.71
Mark's Portrait	1.00	0.00	0.00
Luke's Portrait	0.45	0.52	0.86
Cross-Carpet Page	0.45	0.05	0.14

the 2003 to the 2010 images, counting lost chips, Table 3.5. To aid comparison, I divided the number of chips by the number of years for a period, Table 3.6. For the two incipits and portrait of Luke, these results show an increase in the number of lost chips after 1982. They signal a need for extra attention and care.

Conversely, the portrait of Mark shows amazing stability, as does the Cross-Carpet page. When comparing historical photographs for the Cross-Carpet page, I noticed that most of the losses between 1962 and 1982 result from flaking pigment in the decorative border. This might suggest that flaking pigment was more susceptible to the flattening process, and that flattening increased losses for a period thereafter. Again, studies of historical images for other manuscripts are crucial to sort out these results and their implications.

Before I leave the major decorated pages, I want to return to losses in the frame of Mark's portrait. These losses include both ink and the bright yellow pigment orpiment. I did not include losses of orpiment in Tables 3.1 and 3.2 because they are difficult or impossible to discern in black-and-white photographs. To do so would have distorted comparisons to later periods, when colour photographs make losses of orpiment clearly

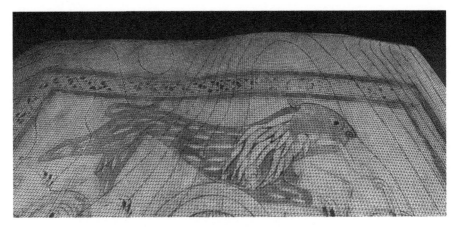

Figure 3.2. 3D rendering shows mesh to highlight contours. Portrait of Mark, page 142, St. Chad Gospels. Reproduced by kind permission of the Chapter of Lichfield Cathedral.

detectable. The frame suffers noticeable losses to the ink constructing its key pattern. For the St. Chad Gospels, losses to ink are rare. However, for Mark's portrait, within the upper portion of the frame, losses are identifiable in all historical images (Web Fig. 3.22). An RTI rendering provides an enhanced view of surface details for this area (Web Fig. 3.23).

Examining the 3D rendering makes the reason for the loss of ink evident. Although it only shows remnants of the contours, the 3D rendering shows that the ink resides in an elevated area (Web Fig. 3.24 and Fig. 3.2 or Web Fig. 3.25). Every time the page is turned or the manuscript closes, this area contacts the opposite page and rubs against it. Before Powell flattened the pages, the pressure from rubbing would have been much more severe, accounting for substantial losses between 1911 and 1962.

As this example demonstrates, 3D renderings contribute valuable evidence for understanding aging. Indeed, 3D provides complementary information in multiple ways. For instance, the pigment of the *M* at the end of the second line of Luke's incipit appears to have benefited from the contours of this page. The pigment resides in an area that still forms a downward slope. Before flattening, it would have been more severe and protected the pigment from contact with the opposite page (Web Fig. 3.26). Because the slope has been reduced, it no longer protects the pigment as thoroughly, likely contributing to why this pigment survives to suffer current losses.

Furthermore, 3D models generate a unique opportunity to view lines of stress caused by cockling. A 3D rendering is generated by combining two elements: a mesh, which represents the contours, and a texture, which represents the visual content.[28] A mesh is constructed from polygons. Because triangles can model the smoothest curves, they are most commonly used, as they are for the meshes of the St. Chad Gospels. Terminology

---

28 For a video demonstration of a mesh and textures, see Endres, "The St. Chad Gospels."

for describing these triangles include the face (surface area), edge (line), and vertex (meeting endpoint of two or more lines). In a 3D mesh, if the face of a triangle is parallel to the surface of a page, the whole face is visible. Where the contours of a page cause the faces of triangles to be at acute angles to the surface of a page, the triangles lose their width and blend into the semblance of a line. These lines represent areas of stress.

Examining these lines of stress help to explain strain placed on pigments. For example, while the *M* at the end of the second line of Luke's incipit resides on a downward slope, lines of stress run through the upper and lower areas where pigment has been shed (Web Fig. 3.27). The lower line runs directly through the larger piece of pigment, lost between 1911 and 1929. The upper line runs along the larger chip that broke free between 2003 and 2010. However, while lines of stress strain pigments, a layer of pigment has its own strengths and vulnerabilities. Therefore, it might not crack exactly along a line of stress. Layers of pigment vary in thickness and composition. Their vulnerabilities contribute to where they crack.

In contrast to major decorated pages, textual pages and their minor initials have aged exceedingly well. Even on severely water-damaged pages, I have generally not witnessed losses. However, two pages are exceptions: pages 141 and 217. These pages are highly viewed. Page 141 contains the earliest known Old Welsh writing, dated as the ninth century. It records Gelhi trading his best horse for the St. Chad Gospels. Furthermore, this page contains an intriguing area showing signs of erasure. Scholars hope recovering text from this erasure will provide information about the provenance of the St. Chad Gospels—any recovered text might prove invaluable. As discussed in Chapters 1 and 2, it has been quite reluctant to give up any secrets, whether through multispectral imaging, RTI, or image post-processing. Therefore, it is a page of great interest.

Page 217 is likewise of great interest. It includes an extra transcription of the Lord's Prayer, appearing below the last lines of Mark's gospel. When the manuscript was made, the extra Lord's Prayer was likely copied for swearing oaths.[29] This suggests that the page was intended for regular use, taking strain away from the Lord's Prayer within the gospel of Matthew. Furthermore, page 217 begins a quire, making it easier to open to. Finally, page 217 is also of interest for its marginalia and dry-point names.

Beyond their own significance, both pages also experience extra stress because they form the recto side of major decorated pages: page 141 forms the recto side of the portrait of Mark; page 217 forms the recto side of the portrait of Luke. Therefore, not only are these pages disturbed for their own content, but they also experience stresses from the viewing of their popular versos.

Table 3.7 provides information about the number of chips lost on these pages. However, the periods needed adjustment. In 1911, the photographer did not take an image of page 217, but an image does exist from 1887, in the *Codex S. Ceaddea Latinus*. To account for the different number of years in periods, Table 3.8 provides the rates of lost chips per year. If the two pre-1956–1962 periods are combined, page 141 averages .09 chips per year and page 217 averages .16 chips per year. For both pages, the rate of lost

---

29 Brown, "Lichfield/Llandeilo Gospels," 59.

Table 3.7. Number of lost chips of pigment from 1911 to 1929 or 1887 to 1929, 1956 to 1962, and 1962 to 2010 for page 141 and page 217.

Number of Lost Chips	1911–1929* or 1887–1929**	1929–1956	1956–1962	1962–2010
Page 141 (from 1911)	0*	4	0	2
Page 217 (from 1887)	9**	2	0	5

Table 3.8. Number of lost chips of pigment per year from 1911 to 1929 or 1887 to 1929, 1956 to 1962, and 1962 to 2010 for page 141 and page 217.

Lost Chips Per Year	1911–1929* or 1887–1929**	1929–1956	1956–1962	1962–2010
Page 141 (from 1911)	0.00*	0.15	0.00	0.04
Page 217 (from 1887)	0.21**	0.07	0.00	0.10

chips declines after Powell flattened the pages and rebound the manuscript. The size of lost chips is relatively small and consistent across periods.

To meaningfully compare these two pages, however, the number of letters with pigment needs considered. Textual pages vary greatly in the number and extravagance of decorated initials. Page 217 has about 40 percent more initials with pigment: page 141 has roughly thirty-three decorated initials whereas page 217 has fifty-five. Because some of these letters have severe wear, it is difficult to discern whether they originally had pigment. If the loss rate per year is adjusted for the number of decorated letters for page 141, the two pages have similar rates, with page 141 showing roughly a .03 lower rate for the pre- and post-1956–1962 periods.

Pages 141 and 217 are similar in that their decorated letters have tended to lose pigment when located along lines of stress (Web Fig. 3.28). When a page is turned, it flexes one way and then the other, placing stress on pigments. Cockling complicates this flexing and amplifies this strain. Case in point, the letter that shows the most losses is the *d* that begins page 217. It resides near the binding. Web Fig. 3.29 provides the 3D mesh overlaying the page. As observable, this letter takes the brunt of much strain whenever this page is opened, flexing one way, then the other, whether opened to its content or the content of the portrait of Mark (Web Fig. 3.30).

Concluding Comments

As Paul Conway argues, "Digitization activities must create lasting value—value that is embedded in the digital collections themselves rather than primarily derived from their association with original source materials".[30] I could not agree more. Digital surrogates must accomplish more than stand in for physical manuscripts. Digitization projects must recognize and take advantage of digital excesses.[31] By their nature, digital artefacts have excesses. They have the power of overlay and transparency. But they also preserve how a manuscript reflected and absorbed light on a certain day. As a manuscript ages, how it absorbs and reflects light changes and cannot be recaptured by consulting the manuscript. Digital images preserve this information, as do historical photographs. Digitized historical photographs return scholars to the materiality of a manuscript on a day long past.

Scholars need to recognize this gain and build upon it, exponentially. One way to do this is to make digitized historical photographs part of digital collections. Digital images, like daguerreotypes before them, overcome barriers of distance and time. Just as early photographs of the architectural heritage of France overcame such barriers, manifest in the lack of rail, so too do digitized historical photographs. By digitizing, registering, and comparing them, scholars travel back in time. They can discover trends, assess conservation treatments, and more fully understand the unique materiality of a manuscript in how it ages. Such knowledge for one manuscript can have implications for others, contributing to recognizing risks and preserving these medieval wonders.

Moreover, digitizing and registering all or a sampling of historical photographs can be a prelude to digitizing a manuscript. While this work will take time, ImageJ makes registering images a relatively quick process. Access to prior images is also generally less difficult than access to a manuscript, whether those images are in books, on microfilm, in archives, or on the web. Methods to digitize historical photographs also tend to be cheaper, whether a scanner or digital camera. For the St. Chad Gospels, the digitized 1887 images from Scrivener's *Codex S. Ceaddea Latinus* demonstrate this value, in the form of a nineteenth-century book. They help to identify trends of pigment loss for decorated initials. Therefore, taking advantage of past photographic efforts, although not as sexy as the latest technological advance, might well lead to greater gains and foundational work.

When imaging a manuscript, digitizing historical photographs should be considered a best practice. These photographs contain irreplaceable information that is paramount to preserve. Once digitized, registering and comparing them reveals patterns and materiality at risk. Information from historical photographs is available and waiting to contribute to the digital age. Scholars need to make the most of these past photographic efforts. Such work is about the otherwise unknowable.

Note

* All Web Figures referred to in this chapter can be accessed at: billendres.com/book/chap3/chap3.html.

---

30 Conway, "Preservation in the Age," 74.

31 Endres, "More Than."

Chapter 4

SACRED ARTEFACTS: OPEN ACCESS, POWER, ETHICS, AND RECIPROCITY*

Being able to compare Codex Vaticanus, Codex Sinaiticus and the newly "discovered" Khabouris Codex side by side from my home in America would have been science fiction just a few decades ago. It is such a thrill to be able to do this. It's like cheating on a cosmic scale.

Will Berry (Manuscript Enthusiast)

IF I WERE TO choose a mantra for the digital humanities, it would be "open access." As a guiding principle, open access makes the digital transformational. It delivers digital content onto the hard drives of scholars and the public. But even when manuscripts are only viewable through high-resolution images, presenting them online radically increases their availability, as radically as the printing press once increased availability of texts. As stated in the epigraph, the rapid pace of these changes feels like science fiction, as if "cheating on a cosmic scale." At this writing, the Vatican Library has 14,623 manuscripts online, its goal to provide online access to all of its 80,000 manuscripts.[1] Yet this is only a mere portion of the manuscripts available. More than five hundred libraries worldwide provide online viewing of at least some of their collection.[2] The recentness of this availability is exemplified by the St. Chad Gospels. In 2009, because neither a printed facsimile nor a full set of online images were available, I travelled to England to study the manuscript. Prior to this, I had relied on a few photographs reproduced in scholarly works and a small number of low-resolution images placed online through a British Library *Turning the Pages* interface. The images were inadequate. The low resolution made features of the manuscript impossible to study. Such features are critical for understanding early Christian and monastic practices in the British Isles. But they are also critical for telling the story of the artistic and scribal accomplishments that lead to the Book of Kells, generally considered the flowering of Insular art.[3] My need for access made travelling to Lichfield Cathedral a necessity, a necessity that if not fulfilled would limit

---

1 Vatican Digital Library (DVL): http://digi.vatlib.it/mss.

2 Through Medieval Manuscripts on the Web (http://faculty.arts.ubc.ca/sechard/512digms.htm), Siân Echard provides links to available manuscripts by country. Digitized Medieval Manuscripts (http://digitizedmedievalmanuscripts.org/app/) provides an interactive map.

3 The St. Chad Gospels is crucial for understanding the development of Insular art, tracing a direct line to the Book of Kells. Shared features between the manuscripts include layered pigments, the St. Chad Gospels being the oldest surviving Insular manuscript to do so extensively. Also, both manuscripts share a square-bowled *q* to begin *quoniam* for the incipit of Luke, a rare design that has exegetical significance.

my scholarship, similar to ways lack of access has limited scholarship on manuscripts throughout the ages.

As a principle, however, open access has complications. The first cultural institutes to venture into open access reported worrying that "the sky might fall."[4] This is reasonable. Anytime a cultural institute, whose mission is to safeguard cultural heritage, changes practices and gives up some control, worries are going to ensue. Such worries originated from a complex set of circumstances, centring on downloadable images and issues affecting institutions and "honouring the artists and their work."[5] Institutional concerns included the likes of proper attribution, copyright, impact on revenue, and effect on number of visitors. Concerns about "honouring the artists" included worries about inaccurate basic information accompanying uses of downloaded images, erroneous narratives about complex histories, and questions about whether digital images were truly up to the task of representing an artefact. For major cultural institutes, although challenges exist because of the continued rising costs of digital infrastructure, those earlier expressed concerns have proven largely unwarranted.[6] However, this may not be the case for smaller institutions, such as a small cathedral library. With a number of important manuscripts held by cathedral libraries, understanding these differences and how to counter potential harm and manage lesser benefits (a digital presence is unlikely to increase visitors significantly to a remote location) is crucial.

Heightening these concerns is also the intimate bond between cathedral communities and their manuscripts. For example, the St. Chad Gospels, a gospel book, is beloved by its community and has a dynamic presence: it still performs its sacred role four to five times a year, albeit in highly restricted ways. To its community, it is primarily sacred. Conversely, cultural institutes view manuscripts through the lens of their public mission, as cultural heritage. Profound differences exist between these two views. Sacred artefacts have rich histories within their community and profound connections that shapes the community's identity. In the case of the St. Chad Gospels, its history connects the Lichfield Cathedral community to its early medieval Christian origins. As prior Canon Chancellor Pete Wilcox explains, "one of the things that makes it [St. Chad Gospels] so precious to us is it unites us to our patron. [...] There is only a cathedral in Lichfield because of St. Chad, and this artefact links us within a generation to Chad."[7] Such connections make honouring the St. Chad Gospels a crucial concern. For the community, it is a centering force, providing a touchstone to thirteen hundred years of history. Through this history and its presence, the St. Chad Gospels testifies to what it means to live, struggle, aspire, and glorify God as part of this long-standing religious community.

A cultural institute does not generally have such a profound relationship to its artefacts. For example, the fourth-century Codex Sinaiticus, one of the oldest surviving Greek copies of the Bible, resides at the British Library. Its earliest known community

---

4 Kelly, *Images of Works of Art*, 23.

5 Tanner, *Reproduction Charging Models*, 43.

6 Kelly, *Images of Works of Art*; Tanner, "Open Glam."

7 Howard, "21st-Century Imaging."

is the Monastery of St. Catherine in Sinai. In 1859, the biblical scholar Constantine Tischendorf gained loan of the manuscript for study and took it to St. Petersburg, where it remained for unclear reasons until Joseph Stalin offered it for sale. Through a public fundraising campaign, the British Library purchased it, the manuscript arriving in London in 1933.[8] The Codex Sinaiticus is disconnected from its community. Rather than serving as a sacred artefact, it is on display, serving as cultural heritage. This role is notably different from the one that the St. Chad Gospels serves.

In this chapter, I explore an approach to open access that accounts for differences between cathedral libraries and larger cultural institutes. These differences include location (cathedral libraries regularly reside in out of the way places), lack of technical infrastructure, and absence of public funding (public funding is reported as the motivating force for early cultural institutes to provide digital images).[9] However, the most crucial consideration might be the relationship of a cathedral community to its manuscript. Therefore, this chapter turns to ethnography and its concept of reciprocity as a guide for digital activity and open access. Reciprocity can provide guidance for counterbalancing any transgressions originating from open access through preemptive larger goods.[10]

Decision and Methods

Defining and promoting open access is much easier than establishing methods to assure it produces the desired results. To understand challenges, a clear definition of open access is necessary. The most widely referenced and accepted definition is the "Berlin Declaration on Open Access to Knowledge in the Sciences and Humanities" (October 22, 2003).[11] It follows and builds on statements by three other open access initiatives, the "Budapest Open Access Initiative (February 14, 2002),[12] ECHO Charter (October 30, 2002),[13] and "Bethesda Statement on Open Access Publishing" (June 20, 2003).[14] The Berlin Declaration calls for the "active commitment of each and every individual producer of scientific knowledge and holder of cultural heritage" to make their content digitally accessible. This content includes "original scientific research results, raw data and metadata, source materials, digital representations of pictorial and graphical materials and scholarly multimedia material." However, what makes open access revolutionary

---

8 The Codex Sinaiticus website, which provides online access to high-resolution images, includes a good history of the manuscript: www.codexsinaiticus.org/en/codex/history.aspx.

9 Kelly, *Images of Works of Art*; Tanner, *Reproduction Charging Models*.

10 Endres, "Imaging Sacred Artefacts."

11 Berlin Declaration on Open Access to Knowledge in the Sciences and Humanities: https://openaccess.mpg.de/Berlin-Declaration.

12 Budapest Open Access Initiative: http://budapestopenaccessinitiative.org/.

13 ECHO Charter: http://echo.mpiwg-berlin.mpg.de/policy/oa_basics/charter.

14 Bethesda Statement on Open Access Publishing: http://openscience.ens.fr/ABOUT_OPEN_ACCESS/DECLARATIONS/2003_06_20_Bethesda_Statement_on_Open_Acess.pdf.

is how it defines access: placing digitized content (such as high-resolution images of manuscripts) into the hands and onto the hard drives of interested individuals:

> Open access contributions must satisfy two conditions: The author(s) and right holder(s) of such contributions grant(s) to all users a free, irrevocable, world-wide, right of access to, and a license to copy, use, distribute, transmit and display the work publically and to make and distribute derivative works, in any digital medium for any responsible purpose, subject to proper attribution of authorship (community standards, will continue to provide the mechanism for enforcement of proper attribution and responsible use of the published work, as they do now), as well as the right to make small numbers of printed copies for their personal use.[15]

Making digital materials freely available for reuse is a radical departure from print culture and its practices governed by restricted reuse and fees. Normally, concerns about copyright and streams of revenue accompany access to photographs of cultural heritage. For example, the Parker Library at Corpus Christi College, Cambridge, in partnership with Stanford University, digitized their 559 manuscripts and made them available online in 2009. For access, however, the Parker required an institutional subscription fee of $3,500 per year.[16] Anyone not connected to a subscribing institution could view images, but they had to find them without the search engine (it was disabled) and the size of images was limited to 516 × 700 pixels. Such poor-quality images were unsuitable for much of anything. Altering its approach, beginning in January 2018, Parker's collection became fully accessible online. This indicates that their experiment with subscriptions did not serve them as intended. As studies by Simon Tanner point out, online access tends not to reduce revenue from commercial sales of images but, if anything, is likely to increase it slightly.[17] Libraries, such as the Parker, need revenue streams; however, subscription fees are probably not the best approach. Openly sharing images reflects the culture of the internet and its originating motive. Approaches consistent with this spirit, such as those by the Walters Museum and smaller organizations such as Lichfield Cathedral, appear the more viable model, generating goodwill and promoting their holdings.

The most common means for providing rights for open access is through a Creative Commons (CC) copyright licence.[18] In December 2002, Creative Commons released its first set of licences. They have since updated them, and at the time of this writing offer a 4.0 International licence. The licences are designed to help copyright holders share their works over the web, encouraging further research and artistic works. The licences are free and written for readability and ease of use. They provide a number of rights

---

15 "Berlin Declaration."

16 Parker Library, through the bookseller and subscription agent Harrassowitz, also offered a purchase price of $9,500, with a $480 maintenance fee after the first year.

17 Tanner, "Open GLAM," 242–44.

18 Creative Commons: https://creativecommons.org.

that can be combined. The basic licence requires attribution (BY), ensuring that the original creator is credited. Other rights can be chosen and combined in any fashion. They include noncommercial (NC) (commercial uses disallowed); share-alike (SA) (any enhancements or changes must be shared under the same licensing agreement); and no derivatives (ND) (original materials can be shared in their whole state but without changes).

Creative Commons neither provides consulting for their licences nor keeps track of who uses them. It is a nonprofit organization. The licence contains the language "if You fail to comply with this Public License, then Your rights under this Public License terminate automatically," but this does not mean that the violating party will cease without the need for legal action. Violations of copyright generally require legal action. CC licences are used widely and generally without difficulties. A number of sites for medieval manuscripts use them, such as e-Codices. I use an early version of the licence, CC BY-NC-SA England/Wales 2.0. Lichfield Cathedral requested that I use this licence to honour the time the St Chad Gospels spent in Wales.

The less predictable result, however, is the way in which downloaded images will be used. Transgressions will occur. The Berlin Declaration is rather cavalier and trusting in addressing this issue, stating, "community standards, [*sic*] will continue to provide the mechanism for enforcement of proper attribution and responsible use." This approach has two major problems. First, the web is open to anyone with a computer and access. This means a range of communities exists with vastly different motives and standards. For example, during the 2017 International Medieval Congress in Leeds, a collection of panels and discussions centred on white supremacists distorting medieval history and appropriating medieval imagery. Although the activities of white supremacists are extreme, they demonstrate the diverse perspectives that accompany community standards and use of downloaded images.

Second, internet culture tends to take a hands-off approach concerning issues of copyright. The gatekeepers have long been publishers of print. Before going to press, publishers check attributions and normally require permissions from copyright holders. As standard practice, such requirements are generally nonexistent on the web. Large web initiatives, such as the Internet Archive, require copyright holders to contact them and make a complaint if they find an instance in which they feel their copyright has been violated.[19] This places the onus on copyright holders. They must search the web, find abuses, and make efforts to correct them or remove content. Web culture tends toward "post first, ask questions later." Wikipedia takes this one step further. It has the "Ignore all rules" rule, which states, "If a rule prevents you from improving or maintaining Wikipedia, **ignore it**."[20] This rule might originate from writing studies, a translation of advice given by the prolific poet William Stafford, who suggests that when struggling with writer's block, do what he does: "lower your standard."[21] However, when writing for

---

19 Internet Archive: https://archive.org/about/terms.php.

20 Wikipedia "Ignore all rules" rule: https://en.wikipedia.org/wiki/Ignore_all_rules.

21 Stafford, *Writing*, 116–18.

print, a system of revision and copyediting generally resolve issues before publication. Wikipedia makes transgressions and errors immediately available, published directly to the web, uncertain if they will be corrected.

But transgressions can likewise occur at the hands of university faculty. Honouring an artefact can break down from a lack of acknowledging disciplinary knowledge. For my project, the computer scientist hired someone to write a blog to promote his side of the work. He asked this person to write an entry about the St. Chad Gospels, a subject for which she had no background. I learned about this entry when I received an email from the then Lichfield Cathedral Canon Chancellor. He had stumbled upon it. He good naturedly described the multiple inaccuracies as "oddities in the interpretation of our manuscript," including presenting the Book of Kells as older and misrepresenting the origins of the St. Chad Gospels.

Because misinformation on the internet is impossible to control, my approach calls for preemptive benefits, that is, benefits that can overshadow and counterbalance future transgressions generated by open access.[22] It draws from ethnography and its long-standing tradition of engaging communities for research. In ethnography, one of the main challenges is to produce dynamic scholarship while protecting willing informants and the community. Ethnographers rely on two consequentialist principles to guide their research and its outcomes: do no harm and reciprocity.[23] Do no harm entails considering and actively working to avoid potential damage to a community, whether financial or social. For digital activity, scholarship such as that by Simone Tanner maps areas of concern and potential damage.[24]

Reciprocity asks scholars to search out and pursue possibilities that they might not otherwise consider, possibilities that benefit the community, not simply scholarship. Such possibilities compensate a community for their part in making a manuscript available for research and counterbalance unforeseen problems. But reciprocity also functions as a heuristic, inviting scholars to imagine and pursue benefits of the digital that might otherwise go unidentified, such as assessing aging by digitizing historical images. Reciprocity makes digitization a more dynamic process.

As a guiding principle, reciprocity is key for imaging a manuscript that resides in its community and performs sacred functions. As such, it is not simply cultural heritage. In performing its religious role, it is intimately connected to the life and well-being of its community. Therefore, a manuscript, such as the St. Chad Gospels, is a present-day cultural phenomenon.[25] From the vantage point of reciprocity, it is primarily sacred and secondarily cultural heritage. This recognizes that any relationship to the manuscript is likewise a relationship to a community.

Regularly, I am asked, what do the humanities have to offer digital techniques? Don't digital scholars simply benefit from the achievements of computer scientists?

---

22 Endres, "Imaging Sacred Artefacts."

23 Murphy and Dingwall, "The Ethics."

24 Tanner, "Open GLAM"; Tanner, "Using Impact."

25 Endres, "Imaging Sacred Artefacts," 40–41.

From my earlier chapters, I hope I have given strong evidence that scholarly knowledge about manuscripts leads to smart choices in how a manuscript is digitized and how its images are presented, leading to digital innovations. But beyond this, the humanities brings an appreciation, interest, and understanding of human relations. For pursuing open access, adding reciprocity to methods provides guidance for developing trust relations and understanding the dynamics of a community and its connections to an artefact. Reciprocity encourages conversations about needs and fears and fosters long-term relationships. From these conversations, exchanges occur that inspire new approaches, spur innovation, promote long-term research, and transform outcomes. It elevates scholarship. But perhaps most importantly, it puts the human squarely into the digital humanities.

Results and Discussion

My results suggest that when reciprocity informs open access, types of access prove as important, if not more so. Different types of access benefit different people with different skills and interests. In approaching access, reciprocity encouraged me to keep the needs of the community of Lichfield Cathedral at the forefront. Whether working through details to make the project happen or designing the website for the manuscripts, community needs remained in dialogue with scholarly ideology, state of knowledge, my research agenda, and possibilities afforded by digital design. Two examples: first, concerns by the community about how the manuscript was aging merged with my interest in pigment loss, leading to digitizing and comparing historical photographs, making knowledge about aging available to the community and scholars. Second, making the manuscripts accessible to the community inspired ideas that likewise benefited scholars. To make salient features of the manuscripts easy to discover, I generated a features page for each manuscript. For the St. Chad Gospels, this page includes short descriptions and links to the gallery for major illumination, marginalia, and dry-point writing. Visitors can easily discover these features, such as the marginalia on page 218 that records Bleiddudd, a slave, gaining his freedom. A recent book, *Slavery After Rome, 500–1100*,[26] references this marginal note and my site.

Open access is not without barriers. Ignoring the need to connect to the internet, which is not trivial for many people,[27] because someone has the option to download images does not mean that they have the wherewithal to do so or gain benefits from them. The size and number of images can be daunting, as can the expertise and expense of software to manipulate them. For example, my full-resolution colour images are roughly 270 megabytes. Each page generally has thirteen multispectral images, roughly 90 megabytes each. Downloading one colour and thirteen multispectral images requires downloading

---

26 Rio, *Slavery*, 117.

27 In 2013, an extensive study by McKinsey and Company found that 4.4 billion people are not connected to the internet (Ferdman, "4.4 Billion.").

1.44 gigabytes. To download the whole manuscript requires downloading 340 gigabytes.[28] After downloading images, overlaying and comparing them requires additional time and expertise, such as loading images as layers into graphics editing software such as GIMP or Photoshop. Therefore, open access does not necessarily mean access.[29]

For the cathedral community, I needed to find ways to circumvent these barriers, barriers that likewise limit many scholars. For me, this is one type of building that is so essential for the digital humanities: envisioning and creating digital sites and tools that enable a range of people to study manuscripts in ways previously not possible. This is access. Thoughtful web design can deliver some of this functionality for high-resolution images. For the release of my website in 2012, I worked with Noah Adler, a programmer, and designed an innovative overlay viewer that allows visitors to choose any two images of a page from a dropdown list and adjust the transparency of the top image to compare them. Not only does this viewer efficiently organize over seven thousand images, but it also allows visitors to recover damaged text and decoration through comparing images, such as comparing the RGB to ultraviolet or infrared, the latter two adept at revealing details beyond normal vision. My overlay viewer makes images immediately and productively interactive, helping the Lichfield community and scholars avoid downloading and overlaying images.

One of the goals of open access is to increase opportunities for engaging digital content. However, copyright holders regularly grant rights for viewing some of their images on the web rather than allowing them to be downloaded. Web design, therefore, can enable interaction and engaging digital content that might lack open access status. For example, I use my overlay viewer to allow visitors to compare historical images and explore trends in the aging of the St. Chad Gospels. For my 2010 imaging, the agreement with Lichfield Cathedral only grants CC licensing for MSI of the manuscripts. Written into the contract as payment and reciprocity, I digitized historical photographs held in the library, beginning with photographs from 1887 (see Chapter 3). Because other institutions, such as the Courtauld Institute, held copyright for some of these photographs, Lichfield Cathedral could not grant a CC licence for them. After research and attaining permissions, I added them to show their contributions.

Assessing the aging of the St. Chad Gospels has been key to my reciprocity. I began this work shortly after returning from Lichfield in 2010. Through it, I have provided the cathedral with critical information for potential loans for exhibits, such as to the British Museum and Ashmolean Museum, including insights for transporting the manuscript, displaying pages, and monitoring pigment. This research provided me with information to write a letter of support for the cathedral in its application for a grant to redesign and build a state-of-the-art display (awarded and built in 2011). Without this information, decisions about exhibits and the manuscript's limited sacred roles

---

28 Endres, "Imaging Sacred Artefacts," 52.

29 The International Image Interoperability Framework (IIIF) is another way to enable reuse of images without the need to download, archive, and redeliver them to the web. However, it requires a whole new level of knowledge and technical expertise.

(such as participating in the Christmas Mass) are made with uncertainty and a level of unease. Understanding aging is impossible without comparing historical images, and this act of reciprocity has allowed the cathedral to make more informed decisions about their beloved manuscript.

But reciprocity also encourages smaller beneficial acts. Sometimes, these are the acts that generate the most appreciation. For instance, when I delivered the final images to Lichfield Cathedral, I purchased an external drive with a British plug. To access images, this eliminates the need to have a US adapter. But furthermore, British electric current uses a different phase than that of the United States. This is noticeable with my laptop: it vibrates when plugged into a British socket. Also, when at the cathedral scanning the 1956 slides of the St. Chad Gospels, I blew an adapter for a high-level US-made scanner. Discussing the problem with a product engineer, I was advised to purchase a phase converter to solve the problem. A British plug, therefore, might not only provide a welcomed convenience, but it might also add longevity to the external drive.

In growing up in the Midwestern United States, I feel reciprocity is no more than treating someone like a neighbour. In many ways, it is. However, restrictions on time for digital projects and demands from teaching and service tend to make the obvious less obvious. Therefore, as if a neighbour, I try to keep the cathedral updated on my research. For example, a year after the initial imaging, I returned to Lichfield to give public lectures on preliminary results and help guide a VIP tour when key pieces from the Staffordshire hoard were on display. In the following years, I have given further lectures, and I stop by the cathedral whenever I am in England. On my website, I acknowledge members of the community who have contributed to my digital work, such as the people affectionately referred to as "babysitters," community members who, for insurance purposes, sat with me while I imaged the St. Chad Gospels. It was a cherished part of the project. I would point out intriguing features of pages to them, and they told me wonderful stories about the cathedral and their lives. I have converted 3D models to PDFs to make them easier to use, installed free software for them (such as the RTI viewer), and provided instruction for software and the website. Reciprocity invites me to treat the cathedral community as partners, as neighbours, and if problems emerge from open access, I have a good relationship with them to work through issues. My hope is that the benefits from my engagement with the community and my digital work far outweigh any negatives.

But pursuing Creative Commons can lead to unexpected problems. In speaking with other scholars, I hope this is not an emerging trend. When working on a digital project, a spirit of collaboration is generally the norm. DH has a reputation for "niceness."[30] This niceness stems in part from the need to collaborate, generating otherwise impossible to pursue research, with outcomes that benefit all involved. For example, my project had multiple mutual benefits. Neither the computer scientist with whom I worked, nor I, had ample funds for a digitization project. By working together, we did.[31] The computer

---

30 Koh, "Niceness"; Scheinfeldt, "Why."

31 The computer scientist had funds remaining from a grant (its work had stalled), and he preferred to spend them rather than return them.

scientist did not have knowledge of or access to manuscripts; I did. The computer scientist had grant-funded MSI equipment that was underutilized; I had manuscripts that could put his equipment to good use. Also, my project benefited a third party and another discipline. Originally, the computer scientist had approached a collaborator, a classics professor, about digitizing classics manuscripts; however, the collaborator failed to secure a contract. By me solidifying my project with Lichfield Cathedral, I justified shipping equipment overseas, allowing the classics professor and computer scientist to meet at the site holding the classics material and negotiate an imaging contract. Finally, my project provided a thesis for one of the computer scientist's master's students, who wrote the scripts and software for data collection. The project was a win-win-win.

Regardless of the mutual benefits, when it came time for the computer scientist to complete his work and deliver the final images, he refused. However, in an email exchange, ten months after the initial imaging, the computer scientist had assured me that he would have the final processed images available for me when I returned to Lichfield. As the time approached, he had me drop off a hard drive. But when I did, he informed me that the images were not quite ready and that he would deliver the images later in the month, when he travelled to England. Needless to say, he did not. Securing the final images took me nearly two years and required me to set up a meeting between us and our deans.

For cultural heritage, final images (and not raw data) are the significant outcome. Final processing eliminates anomalies and corrects variations caused by lighting and digital equipment. For my project, final images required three essential adjustments. First, they required flat-field correction. As discussed in Chapter 1, flatfielding eliminates variations in illumination across a 2D image, including inconsistent lighting and sensors that differ in their sensitivity. In the case of the St. Chad Gospels, shadows required removal. These shadows were caused by the need to offset the LED lighting. Lichfield Cathedral, dating from the thirteenth century, has limited rooms for imaging. Because MSI requires total darkness, it reduced possible rooms to one: the small server's vestry. The offset lighting caused a noticeable diagonal shadow across each image (Web Fig. 4.1).

Second, images required colour correction. This is standard. For such correction, software written for and calibrated to a camera always produces best results. Such software precisely adjusts for a camera's idiosyncrasies. To provide the quality expected of a cultural heritage project, adjusting colour is a given. Finally, images required their exposure corrected (Fig. 4.1 or Web Fig. 4.2). To ensure that visual information was not lost, images were slightly underexposed. Without this correction, images present the manuscript as having aged more substantially than it has, its vellum appearing dark and discoloured.

In a digitization project, because distinct disciplinary expertise is needed at different times, humanities scholars are more susceptible to transgressions. This occurs because knowledge and expertise in the humanities is generally more necessary and concentrated at the beginning and middle of a project. For example, my project depended on me for its conception and existence: contingent on my research agenda, relations with Lichfield Cathedral, and knowledge of manuscripts and digital techniques. During digitization, I was

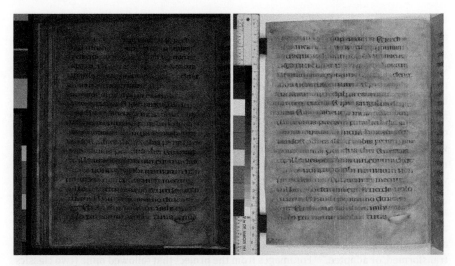

Figure 4.1. Comparison of RGB images, page 90, St. Chad Gospels. Left: Original RGB image combined onsite from multispectral imaging by Bill Endres, 2010. Right: Colour image taken by the British Library, 2003. Images reproduced by kind permission of the Chapter of Lichfield Cathedral.

likewise crucial for imaging, performing a variety of tasks and approving the likes of focus, exposure, and lighting setup. Furthermore, because ultraviolet light damages vellum, the conservator required justification for its use. Therefore, during imaging, I made scholarly arguments to justify ultraviolet imaging when the St. Chad Gospels was opened, and we could examine and discuss its merits for a page. In this way, the dataset highlights and represents my labour and intellectual work, the embodied expertise of the humanities.

In the middle, both humanities and scientific expertise are crucial. As mentioned, during digitization, my labour and expertise were essential. But for collecting the raw data, the project also depended heavily on the scripts and software written by the master's student. However, once images are captured and organized on a hard drive, the last stage is the final processing. It relies on computer science. This does not mean that my expertise was no longer required. It was. For example, shortly after returning from Lichfield, I worked with one of the team's computer engineers to generate a subset of final-processed images, verifying correct adjustments. From this work, basic scripts are normally written, and a computer does the rest. For my project, therefore, final images could have been generated within six months.

Due to the distribution of labour, a CC licence changes the dynamics of a project. Prior to CC licensing, if a project ran into difficulties, the copyright holding institution controlled the images and outcomes. With a CC licence, whoever has the images can use and distribute them to their liking, required only to follow the licence. Transgressions become more difficult to predict. For example, I could have never predicted that anyone would claim that final adjustments would not be considered part of a cultural heritage digitization project. If I had, I could have written the requirement of such adjustments into the contract, requiring them and the final images delivered to Lichfield Cathedral and myself before a CC release.

A CC licence highlights a further disciplinary discrepancy and motive for transgressions. Scientists receive credit for generating datasets; humanity scholars do not.[32] In the humanities, interpretation is rewarded. In the sciences, producing datasets is. For valid datasets, final processing is necessary. This enables other researchers to apply further methods to the images. For example, removing the shadows in the images of the St. Chad Gospels is significant. If they are not removed, the shadows interfere with results when recovery techniques are applied (Web Fig. 4.3). One of the unfortunate aspects of academic reward is that individual work receives more value. The same with grants. This can motivate creative manoeuvring.

CC licensing opens the possibility for some such manoeuvring. For adaptations, it allows the claiming of derivative rights. Derivative rights are generally claimed when materials have been transformed or remixed in some manner. CC licensing refers to this as "adapting." Its language reflects Title 17, Section 101 of the US Copyright Act: "recast, transformed, or adapted."[33] For images from the project that followed mine (two classics manuscripts), the computer scientist has claimed derivative rights. They appear based on final processing. However, these adjustments are a long-standing part of photography. To make corrections for anomalies that entered during digitization, such as shadows or inaccurate colour, are not in the spirit of a derivative licence. Claiming a derivative CC licence allows attention to be diverted from the copyright holder within the copyright notice. This minimizes the visibility and contribution of the copyright holding institution, one of the benefits for making images available.[34]

During the meeting with the deans, it became clear that the computer scientist never intended to provide me with the final-processed images. He viewed his responsibilities to me and Lichfield Cathedral as ending with the raw data. This data included roughly combined RGB images, produced by an automated script to verify pages while imaging. Because of irregularities, the script combined some incorrect spectral frequencies or on occasion produced images with stripes (Web Fig. 4.3). Once his dean saw examples, recognizing the obvious problems, including exposure and shadowing, he assured me that I would receive the final-processed images.

The importance of doing the final processing as soon as possible is emphasized by my project. Because final processing occurred nearly two years after the initial imaging, it was done without crucial information. The two software engineers with whom I had worked at Lichfield had left the university, and the computer scientist excluded me from the final processing. This meant that no one had knowledge to process the images correctly and verify that all of the data was processed. Furthermore, no one checked the final images. Mistakes followed: ten gigabytes of images were left unprocessed, a number of files had errors, metadata was inaccurate, and exposure was left uncorrected.

---

32 Liu, "Theses."

33 Copyright.gov: www.copyright.gov/title17/92chap1.html.

34 Kelly, *Images of Works of Art*; Tanner, "Open Glam."

Compounding these problems, before providing me with the final-processed images, the computer scientist decided to deliver them to Lichfield Cathedral.

As with any problem, making it right goes a long way. I worked with a new software engineer to do final processing of the missing ten gigabytes of images and repair files with errors. Also, I converted 3D models to PDFs to avoid the cathedral's need for specialty software to view them. I corrected the erroneous metadata. For it, the computer scientist had relied on his collaborator in classics. He identified the St. Chad Gospels as Welsh.[35] If left uncorrected, this misinformation would accompany the official images that the cathedral would disseminate.

One of the most troubling issues for the cathedral was the underexposed images (Web Fig. 4.4 and Web Fig. 4.5). It made their treasured manuscript appear discoloured and damaged. To anyone who knows the manuscript, the underexposed images are obvious. It was one of the reasons that the dean had instructed the computer scientist to provide me with the final-processed images.

For outside requests of images, I offered to adjust them for exposure. Before adjusting exposure on all of the images, however, I wanted to consult the manuscripts (St. Chad Gospels and the cathedral's Wycliffe New Testament). This required a trip to Lichfield, one in which I could provide images with correct metadata, repaired errors, and the missing images. Also, I wanted to make the correction before releasing the images through Creative Commons. Once images are on the web, they have a life of their own. I did not want to contribute to any future misimpression about the state of the cathedral's treasured manuscripts, for the public and scholars alike.

Reciprocity might have saved me from a further problem. In 2010, after completing the imaging at Lichfield Cathedral, I immediately began comparing historical images, making assessments as quickly as possible for the cathedral. To do this work, I approached one of the software engineers and obtained an early copy of all the digitized historical photographs. I cannot be certain what happened, but later versions of the 1911 photographs were severely overexposed, making them useless for assessing aging (Web Fig. 4.6).

Copyright in the digital age is unclear and evolving. It is difficult to predict how people will interpret it. The uncertainty stems from the changing nature of photography and larger cultural transitions from analogue to digital and print to the web. This confusion is complicated by the ruling of a US District Court in the *Bridgeman Art Library versus Corel Corporation*. Bridgeman brought suit against Corel because Corel was selling selected images of paintings digitized by Bridgeman. In response to the plaintiff's motion for reargument and reconsideration (1999), US District Court Judge Lewis A. Kaplan ruled that "exact photographic copies of public domain works of art would not be copyrightable under United States law because they are not original."[36] Prior, in such cases as

---

35 Disciplines in the humanities generally respect and seek out needed knowledge in other fields. For example, the Perseus Digital Library, a well-established project in classics, relies on collaborating with scholars in other disciplines when using its digital infrastructure for nonclassical materials.

36 Kaplan, "Bridgeman," para. 34.

Burrow-Giles Lithographic Company versus Sarony (1884), the Supreme Court held that the Copyright Clause viewed photographs as "writing" and thereby copyrightable.[37] This Supreme Court ruling echoes the UK Fine Arts Copyright Act of 1862, referenced in the Bridgeman case. It protected photographs of works of art. Judge Kaplan quotes a modern British copyright treatise that references the 1862 Act, recognizing that "there may have been special skill or labour in setting up the equipment to get a good photograph, especially with the rather primitive materials available in those days."[38] Special skill and labour were a part of early photography, not to mention the danger of the chemicals. But rather than effort or "slavish copying" (*Hearn v. Meyer 1987*), which Kaplan compares to photocopying, he views the law as requiring a "modest amount of originality."[39] For this, he cites *Rogers v. Koons* (1992) as constituting "posing the subject, lighting, angle, selection of film and camera, evoking the desired expression, and almost any other variant involved."[40] Kaplan grants "that many photographs, probably the overwhelming majority, reflect at least the modest amount of originality required for copyright."[41]

As pointed out on the Creative Commons blog, *Bridgeman versus Corel* is "highly influential" but "not a binding precedent."[42] Likewise, it generates doubts about what constitutes elements of originality, creating uncertainty in how to interpret them. For manuscripts, this doubt is not only for originality but also for what constitutes an exact photographic copy. For example, the notion of "exact photographic copies" seems easier to maintain for a framed painting than a page that turns in a manuscript. One of the litmus tests for originality is posing the subject. For a painting, the frame does most of the work. A page of parchment has a mind of its own (dependent upon stiffness, contours, humidity, and binding). Persuading it to lie flat is like coaxing a smile from a grumpy child.

Furthermore, as discussed in Chapter 3, parchment is hygroscopic. It absorbs moisture rapidly from the air, causing regions of a page to expand and contract irregularly. When registering historical photographs, once I adjusted for perspective and size, I still did not have alignment. No two photographs capture the *exact* same image of a page. Its face changes given its conditions.

During imaging, the individuality of a manuscript presents numerous choices and opportunities for originality. For example, by selecting frequencies of light for specific features of a manuscript, do such choices represent a modest amount of originality (echoing choosing film or camera)? Do advanced imaging techniques harken back to the "special skill or labour in setting up" early photography, leading to legal recognition of its photographs as worthy of copyright? Does pursuing ultraviolet imaging for a page, such as my justifications for pages of the St. Chad Gospels, constitute modest originality?

---

37 Kaplan, "Bridgeman," para. 20.

38 Kaplan, "Bridgeman," para. 31.

39 Kaplan, "Bridgeman," para. 24.

40 Kaplan, "Bridgeman," para. 24.

41 Kaplan, "Bridgeman," para. 24.

42 Creative Commons: https://creativecommons.org/2015/01/23/for-faithful-digital-reproductions-of-public-domain-works-use-cc0.

The 1962 photographs provide further questions. Roger Powell commissioned the Courtauld Institute to take these photographs while the pages were unbound and directly after he had flattened them. Having pages unbound is a rare occurrence, the span between rebinding generally measured in hundreds of years. Powell wanted photographs of the pages unencumbered. Does unbinding a manuscript constitute an element of originality in posing? Also, the flattening process involves hydrating, stretching, and drying pages. Does flattening pages constitute an element of originality? Furthermore, Powell commissioned these photographs also to capture his work. Beyond flattening pages, he refilled holes, patched the damaged edges, stitched tears, and increased the consolidation of fragile pigments with liquid nylon. Roger Powell had rare skill. Comparing historical photographs shows that he did not cause any large chip of pigment to break free during his extensive work. Also, his artistry in stitching and repairing the manuscript is likewise impressive. Regularly, I am amazed to find his stitching in places I had not noticed prior. Are the 1962 photographs copyrightable on a separate issue, in that they capture the artistry of Roger Powell?

Similar questions surround 3D renderings and RTI files. Highlight RTI appears a particularly strong case because decisions are made about where to hold the source of lighting as imaging progresses. These decisions are crucial when a manuscript only opens partially. Furthermore, for posing a page, to get it as flat as possible, I use a collection of items, including poker chips and playing cards. By their nature, manuscripts feel more alive than the paintings in *Bridgeman versus Corel*, perhaps because manuscripts are made of flesh, perhaps because they are so well tailored to our bodies. In holding them, they seem as if extensions of us. But until future court rulings make such uncertainties clear, reciprocity invites focusing on something beyond uncertain legal code: human relationships.[43]

Concluding Comments

Digitizing sacred artefacts needs to be about relationships. It can be about power, prestige, control, rights, and careers. However, for dynamic research, it needs to be about relationships. I find no better way to do this than through the ethnographic principle of reciprocity. It encourages researchers to maintain focus on a community and its needs, insuring that digitization benefits its members. This expands thinking about impact that a project can have, many times expanding it in ways that benefits research as well. Furthermore, reciprocity cultivates long-term relationships. As new advanced imaging techniques become available, if a community has benefited from research in the past and a trust relation is maintained, granting future access is likely. For any future work, reciprocity likewise insures that if unforeseen difficulties arise, a strong relationship exists that facilitates finding resolutions.

---

43 As stated on the Creative Commons blog, *Bridgeman versus Corel* is "highly influential" but "not a binding precedent." For curating institutions, therefore, it recommends its CC0 licence for public domain works of cultural heritage "where there might be any element of originality that might give rise to doubt."

Issues such as open access complicate digitizing sacred artefacts. Because cultural practices are in transition, from analogue to digital and print to the web, digitization generates uncertainty. This is witnessed in *Bridgeman Art Library versus Corel Corporation* and the ambiguity and limited nature of the ruling. To navigate the uncertainty, the nonprofit organization Creative Commons provides welcomed assistance, offering a collection of copyright licences to aid sharing of intellectual and creative material. However, uncertainty still exists. I suggest honouring that uncertainty by honouring the people who have done previous work photographing and preserving a sacred artefact. Without this work, important current work, such as my assessing the St. Chad Gospels' aging, cannot be accomplished. While scholars need to advocate for open access, they also need to recognize the people who generated past, valuable work and the communities that preserve and continue to care for these medieval wonders. When a cathedral provides open access to a treasured manuscript, scholars need to celebrate its willingness to take the risks.

Open access opens possibilities for more people to experience and explore the marvels of manuscripts. It should be championed. Digital artefacts are a wonderful thing. They are as important to have in the hands of enthusiasts and community members as scholars. When I return to Lichfield Cathedral and give a talk, I am always amazed at the level of engagement, questions, and insights that community members have about their beloved manuscript. As a scholar, I want them thinking with me. Likewise, I am constantly amazed by the level of commitment, depth of knowledge, and questions of people who contact me from the Manuscripts of Lichfield Cathedral website. Scholarship should never be restricted to scholars talking to each other. It is about talking and thinking with the larger world.

Note

* All Web Figures referred to in this chapter can be accessed at: billendres.com/book/chap4/chap4.html.

Chapter 5

A CRISIS IN KNOWLEDGE-SPACE? A LOOK TOWARD VIRTUAL REALITY*

FOR STUDYING MANUSCRIPTS, scholars have critiqued both text and 2D images. Of the latter, my earlier chapters provide sufficient critique in pointing out material features that normally go uncaptured when manuscripts are digitized. However, this critique becomes strengthened when a manuscript is viewed as more than its text and decoration, whether as a holistic expression or as a socially transmitted interaction.[1] For example, Elaine Treharne points out that a physical encounter is necessary to gauge a manuscript's heft.[2] Heft portrays crucial information about socially transmitted interactions, such as a sense of portability (for missionary travel) or grandeur (for large gatherings). Critiques of this nature recognize that manuscripts are meant to be engaged by human bodies, demanding first-hand experience for knowing.[3]

Although scholars have identified shortcomings in 2D images, they have likewise identified shortcomings in textual remediation.[4] In *Virtually Anglo-Saxon*, Martin Foys demonstrates how textual descriptions of the Bayeux Tapestry reconstruct it linearly, remaking it into a radically different form from its physical embodiment. Such a representation can encourage misinterpretation and flawed conclusions. For a Chi-Rho page or page of text organized around the interplay of decorated initials, the artistry guides the eye and shapes the experience of the content and its meaning. By altering the journey to meaning, meaning is lost and/or reshaped.

With these critiques in mind, this chapter explores virtual reality (VR) as a response to and an alternative for studying manuscripts. It recognizes that VR is likewise imperfect and will struggle to duplicate physical attributes such as the smell of parchment. However, VR represents a profound shift for studying manuscripts. It provides a shared space for a digital encounter, eliminating the barrier of a screen. To understand the significance of this shared space, I turn to neuroscientists. Rather than accept the notion of five isolated senses inherited from Aristotle, neuroscientists have identified twenty-two to thirty-three. They have also demonstrated that perceptions such as sight are constructed using information from multiple senses. A digital technique that focuses on one isolated sense, therefore, provides a limited representation of human experience of a manuscript.

---

1 McKenzie, *Bibliography*; McGann, *The Textual Condition*.

2 Treharne, "Fleshing Out," 467–70.

3 Pushing on my thoughts, Johanna Green and Andrew Prescott have organized and spoken in a series of provocative conference panels titled "Digital Skin."

4 *Remediation* refers to transforming or refashioning the content from one form of communication into another (Bolter and Grusin, *Remediation*).

For studying manuscripts, experience has always been a significant aspect of epistemology. An expanded notion of the senses generates the need to think more complexly about how scholars gather, organize, and preserve knowledge. To this end, I examine a distributed model of the mind and argue that VR provides a richer means to preserve and transmit knowledge based on and generated through experience.

To understand the epistemic potential of VR, I examine historic spaces for transmitting and preserving knowledge. I refer to these spaces as knowledge-spaces. They are ideologically constructed and represent a merging of human, technical, and physical attributes. Knowledge-spaces co-exist, but one space tends to become the most trusted within a culture. Because of the confines of this chapter, I limit my discussion to the Western tradition and the dialectic, manuscript, book, and Web 2.0. I conclude with VR, drawing from my work with the VR environment OVAL, the Oklahoma Virtual Academic Laboratory (developed by Matthew Cook and the University of Oklahoma Library). My goal is to provide a historic perspective, one from which scholars can understand an emerging space such as VR and cultivate its potentials.

Decisions and Method

What kind of knowledge can VR preserve and transmit? Its value has been demonstrated for studying and testing hypotheses about ancient cities, such as assessing whether marble buildings transformed Emperor Augustus' Rome into a "glittering city."[5] For museum studies, VR has long been of interest for increasing engagement with collections.[6] Recently, however, through a 360-degree embodied encounter, VR is proving quite effective in cultivating empathy. To raise awareness and generate funds for its children's relief efforts, the United Nations produced its first VR film, "Clouds Over Sidra" (2015). It provides the experiences of a twelve-year-old girl in the Za'atari Syrian refugee camp.[7] The film is free to download and viewable on a smartphone through google cardboard (inexpensive VR headsets, starting at around US $15).[8] This film has raised twice the amount of previous fund-raising efforts.[9]

---

5 Favro, *The Urban Image*. Two VR versions of Rome have generated insights into the ancient city: Rome Reborn (Bernard Frischer) and The Roman Forum (Diane Favro, Bernard Frischer, and the UCLA Cultural VR Lab). For an example of scholarly insights and hypotheses testing made possible by VR, see Favro and Johanson, "Death in Motion."

6 Cauchard et al., "Virtual Manuscripts"; Carrozzino et al., "Information Landscapes." VR is proving effective for museums, with exhibits such as Van Gogh Alive—The Experience, created by Grande Exhibitions (http://grandeexhibitions.com/van-gogh-alive-the-experience), and Dreams of Dalí, at the Dalí Museum, also accessible through a downloadable VR film (http://thedali.org/exhibit/dreams-vr/).

7 Information about the film and a link to download it is available from the United Nations Virtual Reality project: http://unvr.sdgactioncampaign.org/cloudsoversidra/#.WWj4c4qQxTY.

8 Cheaper viewers are available. For instance, Knoxlabs offers a cardboard viewer for US $7.

9 United Nations: http://unvr.sdgactioncampaign.org/cloudsoversidra/#.WX-dOYqQxp4.

For manuscripts, the lure of VR is its ability to provide an embodied experience of materiality. However, any exploration of materiality begins by recognizing that it is about the human body and how the body engages physical objects—that is, the scope and limits of human sensory perception. As Chapter 1 points out, MSI and HSI are highly valuable because human sight lacks the ability to see reflected ultraviolet and infrared light. Human senses are incapable of perceiving the full splendor of materiality. Their limits as well as abilities structure it. A discerning view of human senses, therefore, is crucial for designing VR. For studying manuscripts, if VR is to provide rigorous and groundbreaking approaches, it must not only accommodate human sensory perceptions, but it also must wisely expand and enhance them.

Twenty-Two to Thirty-Three Senses

While the Aristotelian notion of five senses provides an experiential description of sensory perception, neuroscientists have demonstrated that this is far from reality. They have identified twenty-two to thirty-three senses, depending on distinctions among them. Beyond sight, taste, touch, smell and hearing, they distinguish such senses as equilibrioception (balance, determined by the canals in the ears), kinesthetic sense (perception of acceleration and movement), sense of effort (perception of exertion needed to complete a task), and proprioception (perception of the position of parts of the body). These senses all play significant roles when scholars examine a manuscript.

When examining a manuscript, another finding is also significant: the senses do not work in isolation. Instead, people construct what they perceive by combining information from various senses. To demonstrate this multisensory construction, Barry C. Smith, founder and director of the Centre for the Study of the Senses, University of London, offers the example of an airplane as it climbs.[10] Since sitting on the runway, visual data entering the eyes has not changed; everything in the cabin remains in its same relative position. However, the front of the cabin appears higher. This perception occurs because information sensed by the eyes is combined with information from at least one other sense, equilibrioception (balance), and perhaps data from the kinesthetic sense. Combined data constructs the perceived rise of the aisle.

Understanding the constructed nature of perception helps to explain what is lost when studying images and not the physical manuscript. When scholars study 2D digital images, their senses gather data and construct sensory experiences of the technology rather than the manuscript. Knowledge is gathered about and relationship formed with the screen, mouse (or trackpad), and keyboard. When Elaine Treharne speaks about *heft*, this knowledge comes in part from a sense of effort (control over exertion needed to complete a task) and proprioception (awareness of the position of parts of the body) when a manuscript is lifted and opened, its pages turned.[11] During these activities, maintaining the balance of the body is also part of the sensory experience. Viewing digital images

---

10 Smith, "We Have Far More." Many thanks to Andrew Prescott for introducing me to Smith's work.
11 For a scientific discussion of the complexity of proprioception, see Proske and Gandevia, "The Proprioceptive Senses."

generates knowledge about the body in relations to the monitor, keyboard, and mouse; a sense of effort generates knowledge about moving the mouse or finger across the trackpad to control the cursor on the screen. Engaging digital images produces a substantial amount of experiential knowledge about computers.

The same, of course, can be said about reading a scholarly article. The question for VR is how effectively it can generate experiential knowledge about manuscripts, complementing what can be learned through text and screen. Understanding sensory experience can lead to developing productive new tools. However, it will be incumbent upon scholars of manuscripts to direct this work: the mediated experience of VR must be designed, critiqued, and re-designed for productive and dynamic approaches.[12] VR is not simply a generic thing. A sound methodology must guide its design, one that accounts for a complex notion of human senses, the salient material features of manuscripts, and the research questions of scholars who study them.

Distributed Model of the Mind: Embodied Thinking

New insights into the senses parallel new theories of the mind. One of these theories, a distributed model, expands the concept of the mind beyond the brain and overcomes models that isolate thinking through stringent demarcations, such as the Cartesian mind/body split. A distributed model recognizes that thought operates neither independent from the body nor physical world. As cognitive archaeologist Lambros Malafouris points out, "What is outside the brain is not necessarily outside the mind."[13] Cognitive activity occurs between a brain and things beyond it in space and time, such as people, objects and memories; without which, the cognitive process does not take place. For Malafouris, the borders are so sketchy that there is benefit in letting them collapse, allowing that which is traditionally seen as beyond biological components to become integrated into a theory of mind.

Stressing that thinking is unbound by the neurons of the brain or the borders of the skin, Gregory Bateson provides a beneficial illustration to highlight grey areas existing between human consciousness, thought and the physical world.[14] He poses a series of question about a blind man with a stick: "Where does the self of a blind man begin? At the tip of the stick? At the handle of the stick? Or at some point halfway up the stick?"[15] Such questions defy clear answers. Furthermore, Malafouris concludes that "*brains, bodies, and things conflate, mutually catalyzing and constituting one another.*"[16] Like the

---

12 Peter Stokes, Stewart Brookes, and the team of DigiPal demonstrate what is possible for answering paleographic questions when scholars of manuscripts engage digital possibilities in smart, inventive, and dedicated design: www.digipal.eu.

13 Malafouris, *How Things Shape*, 67.

14 Bateson, *Steps to an Ecology*, 318–20.

15 Bateson, *Steps to an Ecology*, 318.

16 Malafouris, *How Things Shape*, 5. Such a perspective is likewise celebrated by William Butler Yeats in the last line of his poem "Among School Children": "How can we know the dancer from the dance?"

stick of a blind man, a trusted way to preserve knowledge, such as a book, becomes an extension of an individual. For example, a monk with a pocket gospel is no longer simply a medieval monk: he is something more. The pocket gospel constitutes the monk as the monk constitutes it. Together they increase opportunities for engagement and thought.

Understanding a distributed model of the mind invites exploring ways that spaces aid thinking. It encourages re-imagining how to structure spaces for transmitting knowledge. For example, a distributed model makes evident the need to overcome the limited surface of a page in a book. Common strategies include using notecards or having multiple books collected from the library and opened on a desk. Medieval texts likewise demonstrate the need for overcoming limits of multiple codices. For example, Isidore of Seville compiled selections of various codices into his *Etymologies*, including various authors such as Aristotle, Pliny the Elder, Lucretius, and Augustine. Their writing represents what was viewed as the best knowledge of the day. Such collections demonstrate a need for remixing and juxtaposing ideas and concepts for thinking.

This need is likewise manifest in digital efforts such as the International Image Interoperability Framework (IIIF).[17] Through it, a library can make the individual folios of its manuscripts available through distinct web identifiers. A scholar with a IIIF viewer can select folios from different IIIF enabled collections and juxtapose them on a monitor. For an early career workshop at the Eighteenth Biennial Meeting of the International Society of Anglo-Saxonists, Martin Foys extended this technique. He set up a collection of screens in the front of a room (Fig. 5.1).[18] A collection of screens or a desk full of books takes advantage of 360 degrees of embodied experience.

Such scholarly acts provide clues about how to ideologically structure VR. By recognizing a distributed model of the mind, scholars can explore how different arrangements of objects in space affect thinking.

Knowledge-Spaces

How space structures knowledge matters. Jay Bolter and Richard Grusin's theory of remediation alerted scholars to changes in knowledge when it is preserved and transmitted differently.[19] To explore this human engagement, I refer to means for transmitting and preserving knowledge as *knowledge-spaces*.[20] This term aids my examination

---

17 IIIF website: http://iiif.io/. It provides technical details, demos, and list of participating institutions.

18 Foys on Twitter: https://twitter.com/martinfoys/status/891037086018453504.

19 Bolter and Grusin, *Remediation*.

20 My use of the term *knowledge-space* is different from that of Jean Paul Doignon and Jean Claude Falmagne, who use the term to describe a mathematical model employing set theory for assessing efficiency in acquiring knowledge: *Knowledge Spaces* (New York: Springer Verlag, 1998). My use is also different from Pierre Levy, who uses the term to describe a connective human intelligence facilitated by the Internet, intelligence that evolves from the nomadic space of the earth, territorial space, and commodity space: *Collective Intelligence: Mankind's Emerging World in Cyberspace*, trans. by Robert Bononno (Cambridge, MA: Perseus Books, 1997).

Martin Foys
@martinfoys

Following ∨

"Wall of DM" is ready for tomorrow's #ISAS2017 @cesta_stanford Early Career Workshop in Digital Humanities for Anglo-Saxon Studies.

3:46 PM - 28 Jul 2017

Figure 5.1. Martin Foys demonstrates power of IIIF at the International Society of Anglo-Saxonists Eighteenth Biennial Meeting, 2017.

in two important ways. First, it recognizes human senses as part of the engagement, a move that extends one made by Jerome McGann.[21] McGann analyzes a text as an event, bringing materiality into the discussion. As a consequence, he can theorize materiality as part of what a text is and explore ways materiality contributes to meaning as part of the reading experience. My term focuses attention on the spaces that facilitate events of knowing. These spaces can only be experienced through the senses, setting up my analysis of the interplay of space and human sensory perception in transmitting and preserving knowledge.

Second, a distributed model of the mind views thinking as embodied and as operating in space and time. By employing this model, I embrace embodiment as part of knowing. I escape the mental framework of the Cartesian mind/body split. A distributed model recognizes that thought does not operate as independent from the body and physical world, objects of knowledge constitute people as people constitute them.[22] Materiality and how humans engage it become central to knowledge. I am free to explore

---

21 McGann, *The Textual Condition.*

22 Malafouris, *How Things Shape*, 5.

how best to engage the body when it comes to knowledge, gaining insights into potential designs for VR.

In designing VR environments, scholars must learn from other historic knowledge-spaces, whether stone tablet or book. Such a historical perspective aids in assessing salient qualities, limitations, and potentials. Furthermore, it provides insight into transitions from one knowledge-space to another.

Examining ways that knowledge is preserved and transmitted, however, must begin with one crucial recognition: they are ideologically constructed. Knowledge-spaces are never simply technical accomplishments.[23] For instance, the Irish persisted in their oral culture until the country converted to Christianity (mid-fifth to mid-sixth century). Although having developed Ogham (their own writing system) and being exposed to Roman literacy, they remained faithful to their oral tradition. When the Irish converted to Christianity, however, they transitioned to a literate culture. Christianity is profoundly based on the written word. It is ideologically constructed around the codex. Written on parchment, the Word of God represented the incarnation of Christ (Word made flesh), and scribal activity became understood as preaching with the pen.[24] As preaching, scribal activity takes on the prior prestige reserved for speaking in an oral tradition. For the Irish, Christianity primed a wider cultural adoption of literacy. Therefore, technical merit only partially explains adopting one means of preserving knowledge over another. The other and more crucial aspect is how a knowledge-space promotes a larger cultural agenda, its values and ideology.

OVAL: The Oklahoma Virtual Academic Library

In the past, cost has been prohibitive for VR systems. They could and still can easily run upward of one million US dollars. Generally, systems are also restricted to a single physical space, such a Cave Automatic Virtual Environment (CAVE, named after Plato's allegory). However, innovators, such as Matthew Cook at the University of Oklahoma (OU) library, have changed this. Using a Unity3D gaming engine, Cook and the OU library developed OVAL,[25] a VR system that is dynamic, cost efficient, and can operate over the web. Its software is downloaded from GitHub.[26] To run, OVAL needs a computer equipped with a gaming video card, 3D mouse, and VR headset, low-end costing around US $1,500.[27] 3D objects are easily uploaded into OVAL in a variety of formats and from various sources, such as the Smithsonian Institute, NASA, and Sketchfab.

One of the dynamic features of OVAL is its ability to function over the web. On September 28, 2017, OVAL hosted a multistate, multicampus, curated VR class, exploring early ancient stone engravings and art in a cave with restricted access, led by preservation archaeologist

---

23 I discuss the ideology of making, examining it as a literacy in Endres, "A Literacy."

24 Brown, *The Lindisfarne*, 395–409.

25 Cook, "Virtual Serendipity," 147–49.

26 Download OVAL: https://github.com/WalkupAndAway/OVAL-Application.

27 Enis, "University of Oklahoma Expands."

Doug Gann. Such work and sharing are also possible for manuscripts. In 2018, I received a grant from the OU Humanities Forum to build a travelling two-person VR workstation. With it, I will collaborate with other medievalists to identify and design VR tools to experience and study manuscripts.

Results and Discussion

For historical perspective, I examine four knowledge-spaces: dialectic, manuscript, book, and Web 2.0. This is far from an exhaustive list. Because of limited space, I ignore a wider breath of non-Western approaches, such as the intriguing Mesoamerican *khipu*, talking knots. To include an approach that provides insight into oral practices, I begin with dialectic. The importance of dialectic, however, cannot be overstated. It stretches from ancient Greece to Rome and through the medieval period and beyond, structuring education as part of the trivium (the other two areas of study, grammar and rhetoric). While knowledge-spaces for texts are well represented in manuscripts and books, I omitted another, the scroll. It enjoyed a long history, one worthy of examination. Likewise, storytelling is worthy of inclusion. Perhaps second in longevity only to pointing with a finger, storytelling is one of the oldest approaches for transmitting knowledge; its diverse practices, however, would require a book in their own right. My choices represent an instructive sampling, recognizing that a variety of knowledge-spaces are present in any culture at any given time, with one generally becoming most trusted.[28]

Dialectic

For a manageable account of dialectic, I turn to Plato and its prominence in ancient Greece. The hallmark of dialectic is making logical arguments and engaging in a give-and-take. It provides opportunity for asking questions and on-the-spot thinking, inspiring counterarguments to suss out the truth. For Plato, transmitting knowledge occurs only when questions can be asked and satisfactorily answered. If not, knowledge is not transferred. The importance of interrogating potential knowledge through dialectic is seen in Plato's critique of writing. Plato views writing as only able to provide someone with the mere "appearance of wisdom, not true wisdom."[29] His argument centres on writing's inability to answer questions, only able to repeat "one and the same thing."[30]

Plato views the problem of writing originating from three sources. First, context changes. In this, knowledge takes on a new face. Only through questions can this face be known. In many ways, knowledge is viewed as if a moving object: only because its shape emerges from the changing landscape behind it, can its edges and subtleties be known. Second, when Socrates elaborates on the problem of writing as only able to repeat "one and the same thing," he draws on rhetoric's rich tradition in assessing complex audiences.

---

28 Kress, "*English* at the Crossroads."

29 Plato, "Phaedrus," 165.

30 Plato, "Phaedrus," 166.

Training in rhetoric emphasized the importance of adjusting content to an audience, instructing students in methods to analyze individuals and individual audiences. Such analysis promotes successfully adapting words, arguments, and style to the nature of those engaged: "offering to the complex soul elaborate and harmonious discourse, and simple talks to the simple soul."[31]

Third, Plato asserts through Socrates that writing is not "an elixir of memory," as claimed by its mythical inventor Thamus, but an elixir "of reminding."[32] Memory, one of the five canons of rhetoric, functions with invention to generate insight and produce persuasive arguments. As a mere elixir for reminding, writing only prompts remembering and does not transmit anything worth placing in memory. If a reminder is mistaken for knowledge, recalling it provides mere inferior recollections. Faulty memory, therefore, leads to faulty thinking. Writing disrupts for Plato the ontology and epistemology that insured a trusted way to transmit and preserve knowledge, for the present and future needs of ancient Greece.

Manuscript

Transitioning to writing and manuscripts requires a shift in ideology. Trust must be established in the authority of the written word. This trust is well established by the time of Hugh of St. Victor (d. 1141), the theologian whom Mary Carruthers refers to in describing the art of medieval composing: "memory bits culled from works read and digested are ruminated into a composition."[33] Unlike the Platonic view of the written word bestowing only the semblance of knowledge, text has become an accepted source of knowledge for memory. Such an ideological shift profited from the Christian core belief in Christ, the saviour of humankind, as Word of God made flesh. Words, thereby, had authority in a visible form. In the shift in trust from orality to literacy, copying scripture became understood through the oral tradition of preaching, but with the hand.[34]

However, this intellectual shift required more than belief. It required a method. While dialectic provides a method to direct conversation, the manuscript needed a method to direct reading (interpretation). Such methods were generated by the Early Church Fathers, including Origen and Clement of Alexandria. But perhaps no Church Father produced greater impact than Augustine of Hippo, who presented a clear vision of Christian reading and interpretive practices, remaking classical rhetoric into a Christian art.

In *On Christian Teaching*, Augustine transforms discovering and transmitting knowledge through dialectic and into a method of discovery through reading. He describes his method as a "process of discovering what we need to learn."[35] For Augustine, "wisdom is everywhere present to the inner eye that is healthy and pure."[36] This purity requires following

---

31 Plato, "Phaedrus," 167.

32 Plato, "Phaedrus," 165.

33 Carruthers, *The Book of Memory*, 189.

34 Brown, *The Lindisfarne*, 397–99.

35 Augustine, *On Christian*, 8.

36 Augustine, *On Christian*, 13.

Christ and faith.[37] However, central to Augustine's approach is serious thought and rigorous mental activity. It includes a theory of signs, a hierarchy for trusting different translations of the Bible, and a process for resolving what at first appears to be contradictions in scripture by applying literal, historical, and allegorical readings. Through his method, Augustine provides a comprehensive practice for generating knowledge through interpretation.

This shift highlights the ideological construction of knowledge-spaces and the human practices constituting them. For manuscript culture, knowledge is no longer transmitted through interactive questions and counterarguments but through an interpretive reading strategy. Employing a trusted interpretive method turns what is read into trusted knowledge.

Such a shift, however, also leads to the transformation and invention of other practices. For example, scribes transformed practices of rhetorical invention, converting them from a process of mind into a journey of flesh, that is, manifest on a page of parchment. In the ninth-century Book of Kells, scribes employ a *mise-en-page* technique known to later Irish scribes as *cor fa casan* (turn-in-the-path) or *ceann fa eitil* (head-under-wing). It comprises copying letters and words in open space above or below a line, marking them with an oblique stroke. When readers encountered an oblique stroke, they *turn back* in their path of reading. Such turning is consistent with the rhetorical view of the flow of a composition, known in late antiquity as *ductus*, and Augustine's notion of the need to turn toward God during meditation.[38] However, rather than an oblique stroke, Irish scribes regularly marked the text with imagery, generally symbolizing attributes of Christ. In the Book of Kells, such imagery includes snakes, peacocks and lions.[39] The represented attributes provide content for mediation and understanding the verse.[40] This practice guided leaps in understanding, inviting readers to follow a path of interplay between text and image, echoing rhetorical invention through recall and commonplaces (topics).[41]

This interplay between text and imagery functions similarly to the trained minds of ancient Greek rhetoricians engaged in dialectic, working with memory and commonplaces to invent counterpoints. Insular scribes reified this mental process, transmitting knowledge in a vein ideologically consistent with the dialectic. Although such interplay does not occur in all manuscripts, manuscripts operated as treasure troves of memory in a variety of profound ways. However, such practices would disappear with the next knowledge-space, the printed book.

---

37 This health is attained by following Christ and through faith. Marcia L. Colish presents an examination of medieval faith in *The Mirror of Language*.

38 Carruthers, *The Craft*, 77–81. *Cor fa casan* also echoes Carruthers discussion of the importance of "turning" for Augustine in *On Christian Teaching*.

39 Curley, *Physiologus*, 3–4. The lion roaring is found in Isidore, *The Etymologies*, Book X.

40 In the Book of Kells, a lion on folio 51v demonstrates this practice. Meditating on its attributes transforms what at first appears harsh words by Christ, spoken to a man about to bury his father, 'Follow me, and let the dead bury the dead' (Matt 8:22) (Endres, "Oh Lord Make Haste," 217–18).

41 Leff, "Commonplaces."

Book

Being a form of the codex, it is reasonable to expect the book to reflect the epistemology of the manuscript. However, the differences are profound. Although the book is regularly celebrated as a technical achievement,[42] it is a significant ideological re-structuring of the manuscript. Organized by mechanical reproduction, the knowledge-space of the printed book enables uniform script and standard textual features such as spelling and punctuation. As Marshal McLuhan observes, this standardization and uniformity "puts the reader in the role of the movie projector. The reader moves the series of imprinted letters before him at a speed consistent with apprehending the motions of the author's mind."[43] For McLuhan, reading words at such speeds produces the sensation of being in the minds of authors, as if listening to their thoughts. The book, therefore, signals a further shift from Greek dialectic: authors have become largely disembodied and their thoughts disseminated.

Although I am not attributing cause, this sensation of reading as experiencing the thoughts of authors makes the Cartesian perspective of the mind/body split a reasonable development in cultural hegemony. Such a split was already foreshadowed by Christian practices, embedded in the need to overcome the desires of the flesh and purify oneself for reading. Furthermore, while manuscripts contained individualistic spellings that held hints of localized pronunciations, print largely removed them. As William Irvin points out, standardized spellings eliminated differences in the "muscular movements" of the mouth, excluding "personal peculiarities, Cockney, Lower East Side, North Shore, and Georgia."[44] Print disconnected pronunciation from the localized, embodied differences of authors, stripping the body and context from communicated knowledge and bestowing it with an air of universal truth.

With the book, practices of rhetorical invention also shifted. These practices include the role of memory. Instead of insights and arguments generated through public discourse (speakers relying on trained memories and commonplaces),[45] invention came to be viewed as the result of the natural working of the individual mind. Therefore, training the memory and methods of invention were no longer deemed necessary. Instead, the quality of insights and arguments became viewed as dependent upon the quality of individual minds.[46] The social construction of knowledge was replaced by a view that individual genius generated knowledge, that is, the individual author.

---

42 Celebrating the book as a technical accomplishment is central to such groundbreaking studies as *The Printing Press as an Agent of Change*, Elizabeth L. Eisenstein, Cambridge: Cambridge University Press, 1979 (two volumes).

43 McLuhan, *Understanding Media*, 124–25.

44 Qtd. in McLuhan, *Understanding Media*, 125.

45 A trained and organized memory was a part of education, from the Greeks into the Renaissance. A system devised by Simonides of Ceos lasted into the Renaissance, although some still use it today (Carruthers, *The Book of Memory*, 27–28).

46 Crowley, *The Methodical Memory*, 15–31.

However, knowledge-spaces are always a complex intermingling and metamorphosis of previous and newly constructed practices. The speed at which text could be reproduced and disseminated made printed text more adept at approximating a large conversation than was possible with scribally produced manuscripts. Kenneth Burke recognizes this and evokes print's inheritance from the dialectic, describing academic textual practices through the analogy of entering a parlor where an unending conversation occurs:

> Imagine that you enter a parlor. You come late. When you arrive, others have long preceded you, and they are engaged in a heated discussion, a discussion too heated for them to pause and tell you exactly what it is about. In fact, the discussion had already begun long before any of them got there, so that no one present is qualified to retrace for you all the steps that had gone before. You listen for a while, until you decide that you have caught the tenor of the argument; then you put in your oar. Someone answers; you answer him; another comes to your defense; another aligns himself against you, to either the embarrassment or gratification of your opponent, depending upon the quality of your ally's assistance. However, the discussion is interminable. The hour grows late, you must depart. And you do depart, with the discussion still vigorously in progress.[47]

Facilitated by the speed of print, Burke's view of reading and writing as a conversation harkens back to the dialectic. At the same time, however, the book marks a shift in notions of memory, invention, and individual/social relations in constructing knowledge. Knowledge-spaces are always bastard constructs of past and present. They look backward and forward in unpredictable ways, providing nods to previous spaces and generating platforms for leaps into unpredictable futures. But unlike the printed page, which has had five hundred years to evolve, I want to conclude by examining the infant knowledge-space of Web 2.0.

Web 2.0 as a Knowledge-Space and Guide for VR

Far from a mature knowledge-space, Web 2.0 intriguingly veers from the dissemination model of print. Because VR builds upon this model, I will discuss its potentials within this section, too. Its veering required a transition from early practices. As a term, *Web 2.0* was coined after the dot-com bust of 2001. Tim O'Reilly invented it in part to steady the nerves of investors.[48] But before the term, embracing a model of interaction was well underway. Initially, web developers had borrowed their layout from print, echoing magazines and newspapers. However, recognizing that the web was free from the structures of the printed page, they began experimenting with features such as hyperlinks and unrestrained page size. These experiments generated a radical shift, exemplified by the website for Apple Computers. On April 4, 1997, the Apple website

---

47 Burke, *The Philosophy*, 110–11.
48 Davidson, "Humanities 2.0," 478; O'Reilly, "What Is Web 2.0?".

reflects a magazine, presenting text in columns and including a few small images for visual appeal.[49] However, by May 9, 1998, the website is remade. It foregoes organization around text and turns to whitespace.[50] Well-spaced images provide aesthetically pleasing visual information to guide choices, operating as links to available content. While yet in its early phase, interactivity has emerged as the structuring ideology.

Although not manifest, this ideology is further expressed in an animated gif placed at the top of the page. The gif is an iMac. The iMac starts small, with its back to viewers. As if drawing near, it grows larger. When large, it turns and its screen displays, "hello." This expression of interactivity prefigures what is to come: the dynamic transition of the web from an ontology and epistemology of dissemination to one of interaction.

Medievalists have long participated in cultivating potentials for digital technologies, going back to the 1940s and the work of Father Busa.[51] In 2003, because of rapid advances in the web, *Digital Medievalist* was founded.[52] It strives to aid scholars with the expanding technological demands of research, providing an avenue for publication and fostering collaboration and best practices. Indeed, keeping up with these advances is a struggle. However, they afford innovations that produce exciting scholarly possibilities. For the St. Chad Gospels, a few of my innovations provide a sense of this pace: 2012, an overlay viewer for comparing multispectral and historical images; 2013, a 3D webviewer for rotating and exploring the three-dimensional aspects of a page (providing snapshot URLs, annotation, and a measurement tool); 2014, a spectral enhanced RTI viewer to reveal dry-point writing; and 2018, a travelling 2-person VR workstation, loaded with high-resolution 3D renderings of pages of the St. Chad Gospels.[53] Based on technological advances, these innovations move well beyond viewing individual high-resolution images on the web; instead, they provide a means for discoveries and revelations that would not be possible otherwise.

But advances continue in remarkable ways. For example, IIIF expands engagement with high-resolution images, transitioning from viewing or downloading them to enabling their remixing. Early initiatives, such as *Biblissima*, demonstrate IIIF's wideranging potential. One of its projects digitally reunites fourteen illuminations with their manuscript, the Grandes Chroniques de France (Châteauroux BM, ms. 5). In an earlier century, the illuminations were cut from the manuscript and reside in the Bibliothèque Nationale de France (Web Fig. 5.1).[54] Digital reunifications such as this seemingly

---

49 Internet Archive Wayback Machine: https://web.archive.org/web/19970404064352/http://apple.com.

50 Internet Archive Wayback Machine: https://web.archive.org/web/19980509035420/http://apple.com.

51 Busa, "Foreward: Perspective"; Hockey, "The History," 4–5.

52 *Digital Medievalist*: https://digitalmedievalist.wordpress.com.

53 I have had wonderful collaborators for all of this work: Noah Adler for the overlay viewer; and Justin Hall and Noah Adler for the 3D viewer; Noah Adler helping me to extend the excellent work of Gianpaulo Palma for the RTI viewer; and Matt Cook and OU library for VR.

54 *Biblissima*: http://demos.biblissima-condorcet.fr/chateauroux/demo.

Figure 5.2. View in OVAL (virtual reality), page 219, St. Chad Gospels.
Image reproduced by kind permission of the Chapter of Lichfield Cathedral.

have boundless potential given the number of surviving fragments and fragmented manuscripts. Another project, *Fragmentarium*, is developing an international digital library to assist with this work, including digital tools.[55]

With VR, however, interactivity is remade. It becomes an immersive experience, providing the opportunity for a multisensory encounter with a manuscript and its materiality (Fig. 5.2 or Web Fig. 5.2). However, before I discuss full-multisensory encounters, I want to discuss immediate possibilities and benefits. For example, VR eliminates the restrictive borders of the screen. In sharing digital space, scholars can survey a whole page quickly, with a simple shift of the head, even when a page is magnified to the relative size of a building. Without scrolling, scholars can assess whole landscapes, noting significant features such as contours, crucial to aging. They can also view a page from any angle, virtually moving around it or rotating it, no longer locked into the left-right, top-bottom orientation of a screen.

Other readily available possibilities tap common practices or a distributed model of the mind. For example, to explore the Chi-Rho page of the St. Chad Gospels, I can collect and arrange a series of Chi-Rhos from other manuscripts, such as the Book of Durrow, Lindisfarne Gospels, and Book of Kells. All of these pages, even when enlarged to reveal intricate detail, are quickly viewed and compared by a mere turn of the head. I can move pages around and juxtapose them as desired. Furthermore, the VR environment can be populated with medieval artefacts that share artistic correspondences, such as pages of the St. Chad Gospels with sword hilts from the Staffordshire hoard, Irish stone crosses,

---

55 *Fragmentarium* has a number of case studies: https://fragmentarium.ms/about/case_studies.

the Lichfield Angel, medieval jewelry, and Pictish stone carvings. Guided by a distributed model of the mind, VR provides a flexible environment to explore manuscripts in ways only limited by the imaginations of medievalists.

For OVAL, I have already worked with Matthew Cook to develop two necessary tools: one for measurement (Web Fig. 5.3) and another for annotation (Web Fig. 5.4). Measuring is a basic need. Although high-resolution images include scales, they only provide a sense of measurement. Because parchment has contours, two-dimensional images have no way to provide precise measurements. Three-dimensional models do. As demonstrated in Chapter 3, assessing loss of pigment and changes in other features such as holes requires precise measuring.

When sharing the digital space with a manuscript, I found an unexpected benefit: taking an exact measurement is easier. On a screen, placing the beginning and ending points precisely is difficult—no matter the magnification of a 3D model or sensitivity of the mouse. In OVAL, by pointing with my virtual hand, I can easily place precise beginning and ending points. This likely occurs because the action takes advantage of typical hand-eye coordination. On a screen, positioning the cursor through a secondary devise, a mouse, adds an intermediary. Furthermore, in studying the script and differences in scribal hands, I have found that I can measure a large number of descenders more quickly and with less neck and eye strain. For VR, one of the values lauded by researchers is that it takes advantage of normal ways that humans perform acts in the physical world. My experience of reduced stress and ease in measuring supports this claim.

Other innovations worth developing include a IIIF viewer that could be multiplied inside a VR environment, means for overlaying and comparing historical or multispectral images, and post-processing features for recovering damaged content. Because VR enables more natural interactions, a transcription tool might also prove quite beneficial. It could operate through voice recognition, perhaps producing a line of transcribed letters directly below the script being transcribed. This would allow immediate verification within the field of vision. Corrections could be handled by pointing to a mistake and stating the correct letter. If such a tool proves productive, a generic 3D mesh could be generated to accommodate any available high-resolution image. This would avoid the immediate need to capture 3D data for the hundreds of thousands of available pages of manuscripts, allowing these pages to function in VR and take advantage of appropriate tools. Lacking a 3D mesh need not exclude images from participating in a VR environment.

Conversely, developing tools for multisensory experiences, including haptic, will require effort. They will, however, provide the most gain. While possible technologies currently exist, many are one of a kind or prototypes. They demonstrate the complexity of the task and inventiveness required. For example, Wu et al. developed a VR keyboard with haptic feedback.[56] Typically, to complete a keystroke, a person combines feedback from multiple senses, including the kinesthetic sense, touch, and proprioception. For the sensation of touch, Wu et al. simplified the experience. They attached micro-speakers to

---

56 Wu, "A Virtual Reality Keyboard."

a data glove, simulating the vibration of a key when pressed. Also, sound is crucial. The 'click' signals that sufficient effort has been exerted and can cease. Converting multisensory experience into digital form is anything but simple.

For manuscripts, perhaps the greatest advantage of VR is providing haptic experience. The longing to and value of information from touch should not be underestimated. For a talk I delivered at the 2017 International Medieval Congress, I 3D-printed a page of the St. Chad Gospels. When I passed it around, one of my favourite comments was by Johanna Green, who exclaimed, "I have touched the Internet, and it's a manuscript!" The page took much longer to travel around the room than I had expected. A number of scholars took substantial time running their fingers over the contours. When handling a manuscript, running fingers over a page is prohibited, touch relegated to the edges. Feeling the texture of the parchment or rise of pigments is off limits. In VR, when engaging a digital artefact, touch is possible.

For generating haptic sensation, gloved and nongloved possibilities exist. For handling a digital manuscript, however, gloves would have a certain irony. In VR, gloves are more often used to track the movement of the hands rather than generate haptic sensation. Haptic technology for gloves is complicated and expensive. Nongloved approaches, however, provide more immediate and encouraging possibilities. Promising results have come from focused ultrasound. They include generating haptic experiences of geometric shapes and textures in mid-air.[57] This research has already been turned into a commercial product. Based on research from the University of Bristol, Ultrahaptics sells an entry-level and advanced mid-air haptics development kit. While innovation and coordinating technologies are still necessary, the possibilities are knocking.

Understanding haptic sensation also presents opportunities. Haptic experience is likewise constructed, consisting of different sensations, such as vibration, pressure, temperature, and texture.[58] Recombining these sensations can generate unexpected results. For example, researchers have discovered that a sensation of cold increases a sense of stiffness.[59] Similar to visual magnification, VR provides the opportunity to generate an amplified haptic experience. Scholars, therefore, need to view VR as translating haptic experience and not simply recreating it. Directed by scholarly pursuits, haptic VR sensations can deepen appreciation and understanding of textures, something currently limited in the physical realm.

Representing a manuscript as bound takes complexity to a whole new level. However, digitally representing the resistance of parchment when turned would be beneficial. For such representation, a formula could be generated that converts the thickness and contours of a page into a digital experience of its resistance. Stiffness, as mentioned, could be generated through temperature. The turning would have to be accompanied by the appropriate sound, the creaking and moaning of fussy parchment. The research to generate such a formula might likewise bring new understanding about parchment and

57 Freeman et al., "Textured Surfaces"; Long et al., "Rendering Volumetric Haptic Shapes."

58 Freeman et al., "Multimodal Feedback."

59 Gallo et al., "Encoded and Crossmodal."

its composition, leading to improved conservation practices. Research into the digital is never solely about digital ends.

By returning the native three-dimensional nature of a manuscript back to it and to scholars, VR helps restore the wonder of a manuscript. This wonder is generated through materiality. VR provides manuscripts with the opportunity to project this materiality, what Cauchard et al. call "living presence."[60] As mentioned, part of the expression of the St. Chad Gospels is as the Word of God made flesh, a living presence of abstract religious belief. As a living presence, the immediacy of materiality is essential. Heightening this living presence, illuminated manuscripts generate theatrical instances.[61] For example, the Cross-Carpet page of the St. Chad Gospels is high drama. It is a theatrical entanglement of interlaced birds and dogs. It speaks to an intricacy and intertwining of life, impossible perhaps to unravel, echoing Umberto Eco's description of the imagery in the Book of Kells as generating "heurmenuetics without end."[62] In the presence of such imagery, living presence engages with the senses, beyond sight, including equilibrioception while moving around a page and proprioception while sharing the space with a manuscript. VR, therefore, not only returns materiality to a manuscript, but it also returns the experience of materiality to the body and its information gathering senses.

Although scholarship is structured by serious thought and rigor, the best of scholarship generally has an element of play.[63] Play is basic to human behaviour, rooted in learning the most serious of tasks, such as literacy.[64] In VR, play invites looking across a page in novel ways, escaping the trend of left to right and up to down encouraged by the top and bottom scrollbars of webpages.[65] To begin presentations, I attempt to inspire a sense of play and one of its accompaniments, awe, by showing 3D flyovers of the St. Chad Gospels.[66] But in VR, a person can have such an experience firsthand. In OVAL, one of my first acts was to glide along the side of the Cross-Carpet page, assessing its contours. I soon flew over it, swerving and spiraling toward dramatic decoration (Web Fig. 5.5). I learned how easily I could make myself feel queasy. Thankfully, I have built up a much better tolerance.[67] Flyovers provide a quick and comprehensive view of a page. But they

---

60 Cauchard et al., "Virtual Manuscripts."

61 Endres, "More than Meets."

62 Eco, "Foreword," 16.

63 Recently, while reading Christopher de Hamel's "Introduction" to *Meetings with Remarkable Manuscripts*, I encountered this sense of play. As so often happens with academic projects, de Hamel edited his original, playful title for the book, *Interviews with Manuscripts*, the chapters intended as if a series of celebrity interviews (1).

64 Countless scholars have studied and written on the role of play. One of my favourites is Gunther Kress (1997), who demonstrates the remarkable nature of play in a child's ability to learn language and become literate.

65 Endres, "More than Meets."

66 3D flyovers: https://youtu.be/-amOWt4YSzo.

67 In using VR, queasiness can be a drawback for some people. It can require desensitization. OVAL includes an optional enclosure from which to encounter 3D artefacts. By providing a surrounding structure, with open viewing areas, it generates a sense of stability to temper queasiness.

also infuse an encounter with play. Play encourages curiosity, exploration, and openness, leading to learning and discoveries.

Finally, VR needs to follow Web 2.0 in another aspect. Scholars have shown that Web 2.0 is adept at enacting medieval concepts of engagement.[68] As mentioned, Martin Foys has critiqued structures of writing for skewing how medieval material culture is known, pointing out problems with scholarship in "manufacturing the Anglo-Saxon [medieval] past out of the written word."[69] Although the web has its own structures for which scholars need to be vigilant, it also allows for the structuring of medieval concepts of engagement. Exploring this approach, Cecilia Lindhé, Director of the HUMLab at Umeå University, structures key medieval concepts such as *ekphrasis*, *memoria*, and *ductus* into her websites.[70] She begins, however, by recognizing that the digital is not a re-creation of the medieval but a nod toward the medieval, its aesthetics, values, and concepts. Structuring medieval concepts into her sites generates experiential awareness to inform thinking and analysis.

For example, in her cross-disciplinary project *Imitatio Mariae—Virgin Mary as Virtuous Model in Medieval Sweden*, Lindhé focuses on two medieval concepts: *memoria* and *ductus*. For the medieval world, *memoria* is not rote learning. Instead, it is an active process. *Memoria* promotes engaging the mind as a means to invent "new content, such as thought or prayers."[71] *Ductus* is guided motion. In the Book of Kells, as mentioned earlier, the concepts of *memoria* and *ductus* guide the encounter with turn-in-the-path animals, inviting a guided meditation to generate understanding.[72] Through *memoria* and *ductus*, Lindhé provides an understanding of Madonnas. Within an image of a Madonna and Child, she embeds mouseovers that reveal others. By moving the mouse, a viewer explores the main Madonna, connected to the others by colour and various visual and aesthetic features. Lindhé foregoes cataloguing, dating, and annotating to providing a journey through *memoria* and *ductus*, generating an understanding of Madonnas through medieval concepts.

Lindhé demonstrates the value in paying attention to medieval concepts rather than simply physical artefacts. This is highly significant for designing VR environments and experiences. As she explains, "It is not the artwork as an authentic historical object that is important but rather the aesthetic object as a field of potential, as a process, memories."[73] Approaching medieval artefacts through their originating energy—the concepts, values, beliefs, aspirations, limitations, materials, and cultural structures that brought them into existence—Lindhé engages Web 2.0 in a manner to give visitors an experience of the medieval from the inside. While such experiences are never complete,

---

68 Museums continue to explore innovative digital approaches to enhance their ability to engage the public with their collections. For example, see Kenderdine, "How Will Museums."

69 Foys, *Virtually Anglo-Saxon*, 3.

70 Lindhé, "A Visual Sense"; Lindhé, "Medieval Materiality."

71 Lindhé, "Medieval Materiality," 196.

72 Endres, "Oh Lord Make Haste," 217–18.

73 Lindhé, "Medieval Materiality," 199.

they provide a means to connect to the past that complements knowing through other knowledge-spaces.

Concluding Thoughts

For manuscripts, VR is an emerging and intriguing knowledge-space. Centred on inter-activity in ways that harken back to the dialectic and build upon Web 2.0, VR provides a dynamic means for transmitting and preserving knowledge. But it does not simply build upon the interactivity of Web 2.0, it remakes it. VR shatters the boundaries of the screen, providing an immersive experience. Through it, scholars share digital space with a dig-ital manuscript, its three-dimensional materiality restored to it for its study and engage-ment. In this, a digitized manuscript again has living presence.[74]

An immersive experience likewise brings a wider range of human senses into the engagement. Although haptic experiences are excitingly within reach (such as feeling the contours of a page and the rise of pigments through focused ultrasound), other expe-riential possibilities are currently available. They include views from any angle (such as those from the sides to assess contours); magnification to study minute details; having the whole page (even when enlarged) within the field of vision (or easily seen with a quick turn of the head); and flyovers to provide captivating and telling overviews, restoring a sense of awe. For research, some crucial digital tools are easily built, such as for annotation and precise measurement (as demonstrated in my work with Matthew Cook and OVAL).

However, scholars must remember that VR is not a generic thing. It needs designed and built. Scholars must participate so that their questions, methods and best practices guide the design and building of tools. All knowledge-spaces are ideologically constructed. VR presents scholars with a unique opportunity to tailor it to their needs. For this, having a complex notion of the senses and how they construct experience is essential. The materiality of a manuscript originates from an intimate dance with the materiality of the human body. Pigment choice is guided by how the eye sees and constructs colour. The size of a manuscripts is guided by the size of the human body. Human senses structure the experience. Recognizing that people have more than the Aristotelian five senses and that a sensory experience is constructed from data from multiple senses aids in understanding and designing VR for studying manuscripts. A simple physical assessment such as heft combines information from sight, a sense of effort, equilibrioception, and proprioception. Designing VR with this knowledge enables scholars to construct it in dynamic and productive ways for embodied knowing.

As a whole, knowledge-spaces tend to be complementary. No one knowledge-space or collection of spaces is all encompassing because they translate and render human knowledge originating through embodied experience and engagement in and with the physical world. Knowledge-spaces remediate. Therefore, understanding their limits is as important as understanding their gains. But as constructions, they can be altered

---

74 Cauchard et al., "Virtual Manuscripts."

and reinvented. A distributed model of the mind helps scholars to be innovative with these designs, taking advantage of how presenting a manuscript, its contexts, and corresponding artefacts facilitates thinking and insights. During such innovations and reinventions, however, resistance will occur because knowledge-spaces constitute us as we constitute them. Awareness of this basic condition hopefully makes any invention less contentious and instead opens it to dialogue, one guided by a spirit of experimentation, critical assessment, and redesign. After all, as the medieval concept of *ductus* teaches, any expansion of knowledge is a journey.

Note

* All Web Figures referred to in this chapter can be accessed at: billendres.com/book/chap5/chap5.html.

BIBLIOGRAPHY

Augustine, Saint. *On Christian Teaching*. Translated by R. P. H. Green. Oxford: Oxford University Press, 1997.

Backhouse, Jane. "The Female Scribe." Butterfly Crossing (blog), June 22, 2014. www.butterflycrossing.net/the-female-scribe.

Bateson, Gregory. *Steps to an Ecology of Mind*. Chicago: University of Chicago Press, 2000.

Beach, Alison. *Women as Scribes: Book Production and Monastic Reform in Twelfth-Century Bavaria*. Cambridge Studies in Palaeography and Codicology. Cambridge: Cambridge University Press, 2004.

Bede. *The Ecclesiastical History of the English People*. Edited by Judith McClure and Roger Collins. Oxford: Oxford University Press, 1994.

Belzeaux, Pierre (Zodiaque). The St. Chad Gospels, Selected Pages. Colour Photographs. Froxfield, 1962.

Benton, John, Alan R. Gillespie, and James Soha. "Digital Image-Processing Applied to the Photography of Manuscripts." *Scriptorium* 33.1 (1979): 40–55.

"Berlin Declaration on Open Access to Knowledge in the Sciences and Humanities." October 22, 2003. https://openaccess.mpg.de/Berlin-Declaration.

Blanding, Michael. "Plagiarism Software Unveils a New Source for 11 Shakespeare's Plays." *New York Times Online*, February 7, 2018. www.nytimes.com/2018/02/07/books/plagiarism-software-unveils-a-new-source-for-11-of-shakespeares-plays.html.

Bolter, Jay, and Richard Grusin. *Remediation: Understanding New Media*. Boston: MIT Press, 1999.

British Library. The St. Chad Gospels. High-Resolution Color Imaging. Organized by Michelle P. Brown. London, 2003.

Brown, Michelle P. *The Book and the Transformation of Britain, c. 550–1050: A Study in Written and Visual Literacy and Orality*. The Sandars Lectures in Bibliography, 2009. London and Chicago: British Library and Chicago University Press, 2011.

———. "The Book as Sacred Space." In *Sacred Space: House of God, Gate of Heaven, a Celebration of the 75th Anniversary of the Anglican Shrine of Walsingham*, edited by Philip North and John North, 43–64. London: Continuum, 2007.

———. "Dry-Point." Email exchange. July 24, 2018.

———. "An Early Outbreak of Influenza? Aspects of Influence, Medieval and Modern." In *Under the Influence: The Concept of Influence and the Study of Illuminated Manuscripts*, edited by John Lowden and Alixe Bovey, 1–10. Turnhout: Brepols, 2007.

———. "Female Book-Ownership and Production in Anglo-Saxon England: The Evidence of the Ninth-Century Prayerbooks." In *Lexis and Texts in Early English: Studies Presented to Jane Roberts*, edited by Christian J. Kay and Louise M. Sylvester, 45–67. Amsterdam: Rodopi, 2001.

———. "Images to Be Read and Words to Be Seen: The Iconic Role of the Early Medieval Book." In *Iconic Books and Texts*, edited by J. W. Watts, 86–109. Sheffield: Equinox, 2013.

———. "The Lichfield Angel and the Manuscript Context: Lichfield as a Centre of Insular Art." *Journal of the British Archaeological Association* 160.1 (2007b): 8–19.

———. "The Lichfield/Llandeilo Gospels Reinterpreted." In *Authority and Subjucation in Writing of Medieval Wales*, edited by Ruth Kennedy and Simon Meecham-Jones, 57–70. New York: Palgrave Macmillan, 2008.

———. *The Lindisfarne Gospels: Society, Spirituality and the Scribe*. Toronto: University of Toronto Press, 2003.

Burke, Kenneth. *The Philosophy of Literary Forms: Studies in Symbolic Action*, 3rd ed. Berkeley: University of California Press, 1973.

Busa, Roberto A. "Forward: Perspectives on the Digital Humanities." In *A Companion to the Digital Humanities*, edited by Susan Schreibman, Ray Siemens, and John Unsworth, xvi–xxii. Malden, MA: Blackwell Publishing, 2004.

Burton, Philip. *The Old Latin Gospels: A Study of Their Texts and Language*. Oxford Early Christian Studies, edited by Henry Chadwick and Andrew Louth. New York: Oxford University Press, 2000.

Cambrensis, Giraldus (Gerald of Wales). *The History and Topography of Ireland*. Translated by John O'Meara. London: Penguin, 1982.

Carrozzino, M., C. Evangelista, M. Bergamasco, M. Belli, and Alexandra Angeletaki. "Information Landscapes for the Communication of Ancient Manuscripts Heritage." *Digital Heritage International Congress* 2 (2013): 257–62.

Carruthers, Mary. *The Book of Memory: A Study of Memory in Medieval Culture*. Cambridge: Cambridge University Press, 1999.

———. *The Craft of Thought: Meditation, Rhetoric, and the Making of Images, 400–1200*. Cambridge: Cambridge University Press, 1998.

Cauchard, Jessica, Peter Ainsworth, Daniela Romano, and Bob Banks. "Virtual Manuscripts for an Enhanced Museum and Web Experience *Living Manuscripts*." In *VSMM '06 Proceedings of the 12th International Conference on Interactive Technologies and Sociotechnical Systems*, edited by Hongbin Zha, Zhigeng Pan, Hal Thwaites, Alonzo Addison, and Maurizio Forte, 418–27. Heidelberg: Springer, 2006.

Charles-Edwards, Gifford, and Helen McKee. "Lost Voices from Anglo-Saxon Lichfield." *Anglo-Saxon England* 37 (2008): 79–89.

Clarkson, Christopher. "Rediscovering Parchment: The Nature of the Beast." *The Paper Conservator: Journal of the Institute of Paper Conservation* 16.1 (1992): 5–26.

Colish, Marcia. *The Mirror of Language: A Study in the Medieval Theory of Knowledge*. New Haven: Yale University Press, 1968; rev. ed., 1983.

Conway Library, Courtauld Institute of Art. The St. Chad Gospels. Black-and-White Photographs. Froxfield, 1962.

Conway, Paul. "Preservation in the Age of Google: Digitization, Digital Preservation, and Dilemmas." *Library Quarterly* 80.1 (2010): 61–79.

Cook, Matthew. "Virtual Serendipity: Preserving Embodied Browsing Activity in the 21st Century Research Library." *Journal of Academic Librarianship* 44 (2018): 145–49.

Cosentino, Antonio. "Macro Photography for Reflectance Transformation Imaging: A Practical Guide to the Highlights Method." *e-Conservation Journal* 1 (2013): 70–85.

Cosentino, Antonio, Samantha Stout, and Carmelo Scandurra. "Innovative Imaging Techniques for Examination and Documentation of Mural Painting and Historical Graffiti in the Catacombs of San Giovanni, Syracuse." *International Journal of Conservation Science* 6.1 (2015): 23–34.

Crowley, Sharon. *The Methodical Memory: Invention in Current-Traditional Rhetoric.* Carbondale: Southern Illinois University Press, 1990.

Curley, Michael J. *Physiologus: A Medieval Book of Nature Lore.* Chicago: University of Chicago Press, 2009.

Davidson, Cathy N. "Humanities 2.0: Promise, Perils, Predictions." In *Debates in the Digital Humanities,* edited by Matthew K. Gold, 476–89. Minneapolis: University of Minnesota Press, 2012.

de Hamel, Christopher. *Meetings with Remarkable Manuscripts: Twelve Journeys into the Medieval World.* New York: Penguin Press, 2016.

Duffy, Christina. "The Discovery of a Watermark on the St Cuthbert Gospel Using Colour Space Analysis." *eBLJ* (2014): Article 2, 1–14. www.bl.uk/eblj/2014articles/article2.html.

Easton, Roger, Keith Knox, William Christen-Berry, Kenneth Boydston, Michael Toth, Dough Emery, and William Noel. "Standardized System for Multispectral Imaging of Palimpsests." In *Proceedings of SPIE-IS&T Electronic Imaging,* vol. 7531: *Computer Vision and Image Analysis of Art,* edited by David Stork, Jim Coddington, and Anna Bentkowska-Kafel, 0D-1–11. Bellingham, WA: SPIE Press, 2010.

Eco, Umberto. "Foreward." In *The Book of Kells: MS 58 Trinity College Library Dublin Commentary,* edited by Peter Fox, 11–16. Lucerne: Fine Art Facsimile Publishers of Switzerland, 1990.

Endres, Bill. "A Capacity for Wonder: Early Illuminated Manuscripts, the St Chad Gospels, Litchfield Cathedral." September 7, 2017, YouTube. Video 2:36. https://youtu.be/-amOWt4YSzo.

———. "Imaging Sacred Artifacts: Ethics and the Digitizing of Lichfield Cathedral's St Chad Gospels." *Journal for Religion, Media and Digital Culture* 3.3 (2014): 39–73.

———. "Ligatures and the Question of Scribes for the St Chad Gospels." *Manuscripta* 59.2 (2015): 159–86.

———. "A Literacy of Building: Making in the Digital Humanities." In *Making Things and Drawing Boundaries: Experiments in the Digital Humanities, Debates in the Digital Humanities Series,* edited by Jentery Sayer, 44–54. Minneapolis: University of Minnesota Press, 2017.

———. *"Oh Lord Make Haste to Help Me*: Prayer and Imagery Atop Canon Table II in the Book of Kells." In *An Insular Odyssey: Manuscript Culture in Early Christian Ireland and Beyond,* edited by Rachel Moss, Felicity O'Mahony, and Jane Maxwell, 213–30. Dublin: Four Court Press, 2017.

———. "The St Chad Gospels: Potential for 3D in the Study of Manuscripts." November 26, 2012, YouTube. Video 2:36. https://youtu.be/ebr0HNnNNrs.

———. The St. Chad Gospels and Lichfield Cathedral's Wycliffe New Testament. Multispectral and 3D Imaging. Team from the University of Kentucky. Lichfield, 2010.

———. The St. Chad Gospels, Selected Pages. Reflectance Transformation Imaging. Lichfield, 2014.

———. "More than Meets the Eye: Potentials of 3D for the Study of Manuscripts." In *Proceedings of the Digital Humanities Congress 2012,* edited by Clare Mills, Michael Pidd, and Esther Ward. Studies in the Digital Humanities, University of Sheffield (2014). www.hrionline.ac.uk/openbook/chapter/dhc2012-endres.

Enis, Matt. "University of Oklahoma Expands Networked Virtual Reality Lab." *Library Journal,* August 9, 2016. www.libraryjournal.com/?detailStory=university-of-oklahoma-expands-networked-virtual-reality-lab.

Favro, Diane. *The Urban Image of Augustan Rome*. Cambridge: Cambridge University Press, 1996.

Favro, Diane, and Christopher Johanson. "Death in Motion: Funeral Processions in the Roman Forum." *Journal of the Society of Architectural Historians* 69.1 (2010): 12–37.

Ferdman, Roberto. "4.4 Billion People around the World Still Don't Have Internet." *Washington Post*, October 2, 2014. www.washingtonpost.com/news/wonk/wp/2014/10/02/4-4-billion-people-around-the-world-still-dont-have-internet-heres-where-they-live/?utm_term=.afd35b806f4e

Fischer, Boniface. *Lateinische Bibelhandschriften im Frühn Mittelalter*. Freiburg: Herder, 1985.

Fornaro, Peter, Andrea Bianco, Aeneas Kaiser, Lukas Rosenthaler, Lothar Schmitt, and Heidrun Feldmann. "Enhanced Reflectance Transformation Imaging for Arts and Humanities." Abstracts, Digital Humanities 2017, Montreal. https://dh2017.adho.org/abstracts/151/151.pdf.

Foys, Martin. *Virtually Anglo-Saxon: Old Media, New Media, and Early Medieval Studies in the Late Age of Print*. Tallahassee: University Press of Florida, 2007.

Freeman, Euan, Graham Wilson, Dong-Bach Vo, Alex Ng, Ioannis Politis, and Stephen Brewster. "Multimodal Feedback in HCI: Haptics, Non-Speech Audio, and Their Applications." In *The Handbook of Multimodal-Multisensor Interfaces*, edited by Sharon Oviatt, Björn Schuller, Philip R. Cohen, Daniel Sonntag, Gerasimos Potamianos, and Antonio Krüger, 277–317. New York: ACM and Morgan & Claypool, 2017.

Freeman, Euan, Ross Anderson, Julie Williamson, Graham Wilson, and Stephen Brewster. "Textured Surfaces for Ultrasound Haptic Displays." In *Proceedings of 19th ACM International Conference on Multimodal Interaction*. New York: ACM, 2017.

Fuchs, Robert. "The History of Chemical Reinforcement of Text in Manuscripts—What Should We Do?" *Care and Conservation of Manuscripts* 7 (2003): 159–70.

Gadamer, Hans-Georg. *Truth and Method*. Translated by Joel Weinsheimer and Donald Marshal. 2nd rev. ed. New York: Continuum, 2004.

Gallo, Simon, Giulio Rognini, Laura Santos-Carreras, Tristan Vouga, Olaf Blanke, and Hannes Bleuler. "Encoded and Crossmodal Thermal Stimulation through a Fingertip-Sized Haptic Display." *Frontiers in Robotics and AI* 2 (October 2015): 1–12.

George, Sony, Jon Y. Hardeberg, João Linhares, Lindsay MacDonald, Cristina Montagner, Sérgio Nascimento, Marcello Picollo, Ruven Pillay, Tatiana Vitorino, and E. Keats Webb. "A Study of Spectral Imaging Acquisition and Processing for Cultural Heritage." In *Digital Techniques for Documenting and Preserving Cultural Heritage*, edited by Anna Bentkowska-Kafel and Lindsay MacDonald, 141–58. Kalamazoo: Arc Humanities Press, 2017.

Goshtasby, A. Ardeshir. *Image Registration: Principles, Tools, and Methods*. London: Springer, 2012.

Grosseteste, Robert, Greti Dinkova-Bruun, Michael Huxtable, and Cecilia Panti. *The Dimensions of Colour: Robert Grosseteste's De Colore*. Durham, UK: Institute of Medieval and Renaissance Studies and Toronto: Pontifical Institute of Mediaeval Studies, 2013.

Grün, Armin, Fabio Remondino, and Li Zhang. "Photogrammetric Reconstruction of the Great Buddha of Bamiyan, Afghanistan." *The Photogrammetric Record* 19.107 (2004): 177–99.

Halliday, Sonia. The St. Chad Gospels, Selected Pages. Colour Transparencies. Lichfield, 1982.

Hanneken, Todd. "New Technology for Imaging Unreadable Manuscripts and other Artifacts: Integrated Spectral Reflectance Transformation Imaging (Spectral RTI)."

In *Ancient Worlds in a Digital Culture*, edited by Claire Clivaz, Paul Dilley, and David Hamidović, 180–95. Digital Biblical Studies 1. Leiden: Brill, 2016.

———. "Spectral RTI." In *Textual History of the Bible*, vol. 3. Leiden: Brill (forthcoming). May 2017 version http://jubilees.stmarytx.edu/Hanneken(2017)SpectralRTI(BrillTHB3).html.

Haseldens, Reginald Berti. *Scientific Aids for the Study of Manuscripts*. Supplement to the Bibliographical Society's Transactions, No. 10. Oxford: Oxford University Press, 1935: 71–72.

Hockey, Susan. "The History of Humanities Computing." In *A Companion to the Digital Humanities*, edited by Susan Schreibman, Ray Siemens, and John Unsworth, 3–19. Malden, MA: Blackwell Publishing, 2004.

Hollaus, Fabian, Melanie Gau, and Robert Sablatnig. "Multispectral Image Acquisition of Ancient Manuscripts." In *Progress in Cultural Heritage Preservation, EuroMed 2012*, edited by M. Ioannides et al., 30–39. Berlin: Springer, 2012.

Hopkins-James, Lemuel. *The Celtic Gospels: The Story and Their Text*. Oxford: Oxford University Press, 1934.

Howard, Jennifer. "21st-Century Imaging Helps Scholars Reveal Rare 8th-Century Manuscript." *The Chronicle of Higher Education* (December 5, 2010): A8, A10.

Isidore of Seville. *The Etymologies of Isidore of Seville*, edited by Stephen Barney and translated by W. J. Lewis, J. A. Beach, and Oliver Berghof. Cambridge: Cambridge University Press, 2006.

James, Pamela. "The Lichfield Gospels: The Question of Provenance." *Parergon* 13.2 (1996): 51–61.

Jenkins, Dafydd, and Morfydd E. Owen. "The Welsh Marginalia in the Lichfield Gospels," Part I. *Cambridge Medieval Celtic Studies* 5 (1983): 37–66.

Kaplan, Lewis A. "Bridgeman Art Library, Ltd. V. Corel Corp., 36 F. Supp. 2d 191 (S.D.N.Y. 1999)." Cornell Law School. www.law.cornell.edu/copyright/cases/36_FSupp2d_191.htm.

Kelly, Kristen. *Images of Works of Art in Museum Collections: The Experience of Open Access*. A Study of 11 Museums. New York: Andrew W. Mellon Foundation, 2013.

Kenderdine, Sarah. "How Will Museums of the Future Look?" *TEdxGateway 2013*, YouTube. Video, 13:44. https://youtu.be/VXhtwFCA_Kc.

Kiernan, Kevin. "Digital Image Processing and the *Beowulf* Manuscript." *Literary and Linguistic Computing* 6.1 (1991): 20–27.

Koh, Adeline. "Niceness, Building, and Opening the Genealogy of the Digital Humanities: Beyond the Social Contract of Humanities Computing." *differences: A Journal of Feminist Cultural Studies* 25.1 (2014): 93–106.

Kress, Gunther. *Before Writing: Rethinking the Paths to Literacy*. London: Routledge, 1997.

———. "*English* at the Crossroads: Rethinking Curricula of Communication in the Context of the Turn to the Visual." In *Passions, Pedagogies, and 21st Century Technologies*, edited by Gale Hawisher and Cynthia Selfe, 66–88. Logan: Utah State University Press, 1999.

Kwakkel, Erik. "Doodles in Medieval Manuscripts." In *medievalbooks* (blog), October 5, 2018. https://medievalbooks.nl/2018/10/05/doodles-in-medieval-manuscripts.

———. "Filling a Void: The Use of Marginal Space in Medieval Books." In *Reactions: Medieval/ Modern*, edited by Dot Porter, 19–30. Philadelphia: University of Pennsylvania Libraries, 2016.

Leff, Michael. "Commonplaces and Argumentation in Cicero and Quintilian." *Argumentation* 10 (1996): 445–52.

Lindhé, Cecilia. "Medieval Materiality through the Digital Lens." In *Between Humanities and the Digital*, edited by Patrik Swensson and David Theo Goldberg, 193–204. Boston: MIT Press, 2015.

———. "'A Visual Sense Is Born in the Fingertips': Towards a Digital Ekphrasis." *Digital Humanities Quarterly* 7.1 (2013). www.digitalhumanities.org/dhq/vol/7/1/000161/000161.html.

Liu, Alan. "Theses on the Epistemology of the Digital: Advice for the Cambridge Centre for Digital Knowledge." August 14, 2014. http://liu.english.ucsb.edu/theses-on-the-epistemology-of-the-digital-page.

Llyfrgell Genedlaethol Cymru/The National Library of Wales. The St. Chad Gospels. Photostat Copy, 1929.

Long, Benjamin, Sue Ann Seah, Tom Carter, and Sriram Subramanian. "Rendering Volumetric Haptic Shapes in Mid-Air Using Ultrasound." *ACM Transactions on Graphics* 33.6, Article 181 (2014): 1–10.

Lowe, E. A. *Codices Latini Antiquiores: A Palaeographical Guide to Latin Manuscripts Prior to the Ninth Century, Part II, Great Britain and Ireland*. Oxford: Clarendon Press, 1972.

MacDonald, Lindsay, John Hindmarch, Stuart Robson, and Melissa Terras. "Modelling the Appearance of Heritage Metallic Surfaces." In *ISPRS—International Archives of the Photogrammetry, Remote Sensing and Spatial Information Sciences*, XL.5 (2014): 337–77.

Malafouris, Lambros. *How Things Shape the Mind: A Theory of Material Engagement*. Cambridge, MA: MIT Press, 2013.

Malzbender, Tom, Dan Gelb, and Hans Wolters. "Polynomial Texture Maps." ACM SIGGRAPH 2001 Proceedings. New York: Association for Computing Machinery (2001): 519–28.

McGann, Jerome. *The Textual Condition*. Princeton: Princeton University Press, 1991.

McKenzie, D. F. *Bibliography and Sociology of the Text*. Cambridge: Cambridge University Press, 1999.

McLuhan, Marshall. *Understanding Media: The Extensions of Man*. Cambridge, MA: MIT Press, 1964.

McNamara, Martin. "Irish Gospel Texts, Amb. 1.61 Sup., Bible Text and Date of Kells." In *The Book of Kells: Proceedings of a Conference at Trinity College, Dublin, 6–9 September 1992*, edited by Felicity O'Mahony, 78–101. Aldershot: Scholar Press, 1994.

Meehan, Bernard. *The Book of Kells*. New York: Thames & Hudson, 2012.

Mitchell, C. Ainsworth, and T. C. Hepworth. *Inks: Their Composition and Manufacture*. 2nd ed. London: Charles Griffin, 1916.

Murphy, Elizabeth, and Robert Dingwall. "The Ethics of Ethnography." In *Handbook of Ethnography*, edited by Paul Atkins and Sara Delamont, 339–51. London: Sage, 2001.

Murphy, Patrick. *Unriddling the Exeter Riddles*. University Park: Pennsylvania State University Press, 2011.

Obrutcky, Alba, and Daniel Acosta. "Reflectography, a NDT Method for Images Diagnosis." In *Proceedings of 16th World Conference on Nondestructive Testing*, 46–51, 2004. www.ndt.net/abstract/wcndt2004/740.htm.

O'Reilly, Tim. "What Is Web 2.0? Design Patterns and Business Models for the Next Generation of Software." *O'Reilly Media*. September 30, 2005. www.oreilly.com/pub/a/web2/archive/ what-is-web-20.html.

Oslender, Frowin, Br. (Maria Laach). The St. Chad Gospels, Selected Pages. Colour Slides. Lichfield, c. 1956.

Pataki-Hundt, Andrea. "Conservation Treatment and Stabilization of the Ninth-Century Stuttgart Psalter." *Journal of the Institute of Conservation* 35.2 (2012): 152–64.

Plato. "Phaedrus." In *The Rhetorical Tradition: Reading from Classical Times to the Present*, 2nd ed., translated by H. N. Fowler, 138–69. Boston: Bedford/St. Martin's, 2001.

Powell, Roger. "The Lichfield St. Chad's Gospels: Repair and Rebinding, 1961–1962." *The Library*, Fifth Series, 20.4 (1965): 259–65.

Proske, Uwe, and Simon C. Gandevia. "The Proprioceptive Senses: Their Roles in Signaling Body Shape, Body Position and Movement, and Muscle Force." *Physiological Reviews* 92 (2012): 1651–97.

Rio, Alice. *Slavery After Rome, 500–1100*. Oxford Studies in Medieval European History. Oxford: Oxford University Press, 2017.

Roosen-Rung, Heinz, and A. E. A. Werner, "The Pictorial Technique of the Lindisfarne Gospels." In *Codex Lindisfarnensis*, vol. 2, edited by T. D. Kendrick, 261–77. Olten: Urs Graf, 1960.

Rueden, Curtis, Johannes Schindelin, Mark Hiner, Barry DeZonia, Alison Walter, Ellen Arena, and Kevin Eliceiri. "ImageJ2: ImageJ for the Next Generation of Scientific Image Data." *BMC Bioinformatics* 18.529 (2017): 529–55.

Scheinfeldt, Tom. "Why Digital Humanities Is *Nice*." In *Debates in the Digital Humanities*, edited by Matthew Gold, 59–60. Minneapolis: University of Minnesota Press, 2012.

Schindelin, Johannes, Curtis Rueden, Mark Hiner, and Kevin Eliceiri. "The ImageJ Ecosystem: An Open Platform for Biomedical Image Analysis." *Molecular Reproduction & Development* 82.512 (2015): 518–29.

Schuler, Irmgard. "The Use of Photography for Manuscript Preservation," Paper, IFLA Satellite Meeting: Conservation and Preservation of Library Material in a Cultural-Heritage Oriented Context, Rome, 2009. www.ifla.org/files/assets/pac/Satellite_Meeting_Rome_ 2009/Schuler_eng.pdf.

Scrivener, Fredrick Henry Ambrose. *Codex S. Ceaddea Latinus: evangelia SSS. Matthaei, Marci, Lucae ad cap. III. 9 complectens, circa septimum vel octavum saeculum scriptus, in ecclesia cathedrali Lichfieldiensi servatus*. Cantabrigiae: C. J. Clay, 1887.

Shiel, Patrick, Malte Rehbein, and John Keating. "The Ghost in the Manuscript: Hyperspectral Text Recovery and Segmentation." In *Codicology and Palaeography in the Digital Age*, edited by Malte Rehbein, Patrick Sahle, and Torsten Schassan, 159–74. Norderstedt: Books on Demand, 2009.

Smith, Albert Hugh. "The Photography of Manuscripts." *London Mediaeval Studies* 1 (1938): 179–207.

Smith, Barry C. "We Have Far More Than Five Senses." Video, 5:35. https://youtu.be/ zWdfpwCghIw.

Snijders, Ludo, Tim Zaman, and David Howell. "Using Hyperspectral Imaging to Reveal a Hidden Precolonial Mesoamerican Codes." *Journal of Archaeological Science: Reports* 9 (2016): 143–49.

Speta, Birgit. "The Conservation of the Hussite Codex (Mus. Hs. 15492)." In *Paper Conservation: Decisions & Compromises*, edited by Lieve Watteeuw and Christa Hofmann, 21–23. ICOM-CC Graphic Document Working Group, Interim Meeting. Vienna: International Council of Museums, 2013.

Stafford, William. *Writing the Australian Crawl: Views on the Writer's Vocation*. Ann Arbor: University of Michigan Press, 1978.

Stein, Wendy. *The Lichfield Gospels*. PhD diss., University of California, Berkeley, 1980.

Stolow, Nathan. *Conservation and Exhibitions: Packing, Transport, Storage, and Environmental Consideration*. Butterworths Series in Conservation and Museology. London: Butterworth, 1987.

Tanner, Simon. "Open GLAM: The Reward (and Some Risks) of Digital Sharing for the Public Good." In *Display at Your Own Risk: An Experimental Exhibition of Digital Cultural Heritage*, edited by Andrea Wallace and Ronan Deazley, 239–47. London: King's College London Research Portal, 2016. https://kclpure.kcl.ac.uk/portal/en/publications/open-glam-the-rewards-and-some-risks-of-digital-sharing-for-the-public-good(aacee7d4-8acc-46aa-a73c-d3650fbd3868).html.

———. *Reproduction Charging Models & Rights Policy for Digital Images in American Art Museums: A Mellon Foundation Funded Study*. London: King's College London, 2004.

———. "Using Impact as a Strategic Tool for Developing the Digital Library via the Balance Value Impact Model." *Library Leadership & Management* 30.4 (2016): 1–16.

Treharne, Elaine. "'Fleshing Out the Text': The Transcendent Manuscript in the Digital Age." *Postmedieval* 4.4 (2013): 465–78.

University of Cambridge Research. "Ghosts from the Past Brought Back to Life." April 1, 2015. www.cam.ac.uk/research/news/ghosts-from-the-past-brought-back-to-life.

van den Elsen, Petra, Evert-Jan C. Pol, and Max A Viergever. "Medical Imaging Matching—A Review with Classification." *IEEE Engineering in Medicine and Biology* (1993): 26–39.

Watteeuw, Lieve, Hendrik Hameeuw, Bruno Vandermeulen, Athena Van der Peere, Vanessa Boschloos, Luc Delvaux, Marc Proesmans, Marina Van Bos, and Luc Van Gool. "Light, Shadows and Surface Characteristics: The Multispectral Portable Light Dome." *Applied Physics A* 122.976 (2016). https://doi.org/10.1007/s00339-016-0499-4.

Woods, Chris. "Conservation Treatments for Parchment Documents." *Journal of the Society of Archivists* 16.2 (1995): 221–38.

Wu, Chien-Min, Chih-Wen Hsu, Tzu-Kuei Lee, and Shana Smith. "A Virtual Reality Keyboard with Realistic Haptic Feedback in a Fully Immersive Virtual Environment." *Virtual Reality* 21 (2017): 19–29.

INDEX

Printed and bound by CPI Group (UK) Ltd, Croydon, CR0 4YY

16/04/2025

14658358-0001